# THE WIZARD OF OZ
## and
## WHO HE WAS

L. FRANK BAUM

# THE WIZARD OF OZ
## and
# WHO HE WAS

MARTIN GARDNER AND RUSSEL B. NYE, EDITORS

MICHIGAN STATE UNIVERSITY PRESS

EAST LANSING

1994

All Michigan State University Press books are produced on paper which meets
the requirements of American National Standard of Information Sciences—
Permanence of paper for printed materials ANSI Z39.48-1984.

Library of Congress Catalog Card Number 56-8022

ISBN 0-87013-366-7

Michigan State University Press
East Lansing , Michigan  48823-5202

# Contents

# *Acknowledgments*

The editors wish to thank the following persons: Frank J. Baum, son of L. Frank Baum, for supplying numerous details about his father's life; Roland Baughman, head of the special collections department, Columbia University Libraries, for additions to the bibliography and for his great generosity in loaning a copy of the first edition of *The Wonderful Wizard of Oz* for the reproduction of certain of the original Denslow illustrations for this book; Anthony Boucher, editor of *Fantasy and Science Fiction,* for permission to reprint a heavily revised and expanded version of "The Royal Historian of Oz," which first appeared in the January and February 1955 issues of his magazine; C. Beecher Hogan, lecturer in English at Yale University, for aid in the preparation of the bibliography; Fred Meyer, of Kinderhook, Illinois, for many valuable suggestions; and the late Jack Snow for providing the frontispiece photograph, the poster reproduced on the jacket, and much information about Baum's life and writings.

# *Introduction*

In 1957 popular culture was not yet an acceptable academic discipline: a Pulitzer prize-winning scholar would, in those days, have been expected to concern himself with weightier matters. Russel Nye, however, was a different kind of scholar, a scholar whose Jeffersonian political ideals extended beyond politics into a popular culture that others were denouncing as "middlebrow." When Nye teamed up with Martin Gardner to bring out a new edition of L. Frank Baum's children's classic *The Wizard of Oz and Who He Was* the politics of culture came briefly into focus.

Martin Gardner in his introduction to the new edition addressed the question of "who he was" with a brief biographical essay on Baum. Lyman Frank Baum, we learn from Gardner, was born in 1856 near Syracuse, New York. He began his writing career in 1875 by founding the *New Era*, a newspaper still published in Bradford, Pennsylvania. He went on to manage opera houses, act in the theater, and establish a magazine for window dressers. In 1900 he wrote the first of *The Wonderful Wizard of Oz* books. Its popularity kept him writing Oz books for the rest of his life: and even beyond his life, for after he died in 1919 others were commissioned to write more books about the Wizard. Clearly, Baum was an American original, a gifted writer and a flamboyant promoter. In 1905 he purchased Pedloe Island off the coast of California and announced plans to build a miniature land of Oz for children. What might have been America's first theme park was never built, but Baum's Oz film company founded in 1914 did produce some silent screen versions of his tales.

THE WIZARD OF OZ

The 1939 film, starring Judy Garland, Ray Bolger, and Bert Lahr, was, in fact, the third film presentation of Oz.

Russel Nye's contribution to the new edition, aptly titled an "appreciation," was a masterful combination of enthusiasm and scholarship, an overview of the world Baum created in fifteen admittedly uneven stories. Nye heard the echoes of Ben Franklin in Baum's voice and noted specifically American virtues blended with European fairy-tale tradition. Nye's praise of Baum was tempered, however, by restraint and precision: he fairly acknowledged Baum's limitations, as well as his gifts. Baum's most unique gift, his uncanny understanding of children, explains, Nye noted, his failure to achieve critical or official popularity among the professional arbiters of children's literature. The absence of overt moralizing provided parents with "little help in adjusting and civilizing the young."

The writer's understanding of children is one that the scholar seems to have shared. Commenting on Baum's subtle and gentle humor, for example, Nye confidently predicted that children would enjoy the humor "if adults can be prevented from explaining the joke." It should be noted, then, that Nye's "appreciation" of Baum is, most refreshingly, an appreciation of children, their needs, their joys, and, above all, their intelligence.

The urge to adjust and civilize was, it turned out, as compelling in 1957 as it had been years before when *The Wonderful Wizard of Oz* first appeared. When the Michigan State University Press published Nye and Gardner's new edition with the original illustrations of W. W. Denslow no one expected that this children's book would become a battlefield of clashing viewpoints.

The director of the Detroit Library, one Ralph Ulveling, triggered the battle when he attended a librarians' conference at Kellogg Center. It had long been rumored that the Detroit library had been censoring books and Ulveling in his remarks about the Wizard seemed to confirm the rumors. Addressing the conference on April 3, 1957, or, as he later claimed, responding to a reporter's question about *The Wizard of Oz*, Ulveling criticized the books for their "negativism." "Instead of setting a high goal," he continued, "it drags young minds down to a cowardly level." The Oz books, he

*Introduction*

added, were old-fashioned and inferior to "the modern books we stock." Although he acknowledged that there had been some demand for the book after the 1939 movie, he assured his audience that "kids don't complain."

Ulveling's anti-Oz comments might have gone unnoticed if the *Lansing State Journal*'s staff reporter Neil Hunter hadn't featured his remarks under the headline "Librarian raps Oz books." Aroused by the ugly odor of censorship, Lyle Blair, the director of Michigan State University's press, and Professor Nye responded rapidly with a press conference to defend the children's classic. Blair defended the book as "a great American literary work," and Nye remarked that, "If the message of the Oz books—that love, kindness and unselfishness make the world a better place was, as Ulveling said, of no value today, we should reassess a good many other things about our modern society besides the Detroit Library's approved list of children's books."

The United Press wires sent the story across the nation and America's leading literary newspapers and magazines leapt to the defense of the Wizard. On April 28, 1957, the *Boston Herald*'s commentator, the noted historian of the novel, Edward Wagenknecht, hoped that the book's success would encourage Nye and Gardner to write a complete biography of Baum. The *Washington Post* picked up the story on the same day and, after giving Ulveling some lumps, predicted that Nye's prestige would rescue the Wizard from his enemies. Even conservative publications like the *Wall Street Journal* and William F. Buckley's *National Review* defended the Wizard. On May 1 the *Wall Street Journal*, quoting Martin Gardner, declared that Baum was "America's greatest writer of children's stories, as everyone knows except librarians and writers of juvenile literature." On May 25, the anonymous editorialist of the *National Review*, displaying a Buckleyesque waggishness, issued a playful warning and threatened to turn Mr. Ulveling into "an ass." The writer added that the citizens of Detroit "having a deficient imagination will probably look at Mr. Ulveling and fail to see the change."

While the *National Review* threatened to change Mr. Ulveling into an ass, Anthony Boucher, writing in the August issue of *The*

*Magazine of Fantasy and Fiction*, tried to turn him into a verb. "Ulvel," as Boucher defined it, was "to homogenize; to render tasteless; to reduce to an indistinguishable and insipid mass; to apply such a process particularly to literature." "Ulvel" never caught on as a verb and Ralph Ulveling failed to achieve the infamy of William Bowlder, the nineteenth century purifier of texts, but he was provoked into launching a counter-attack in *The American Library Bulletin*. The whole "alleged controversy," Ulveling charged, "had all the ingredients of a publicity hoax." His library's policy was to let copies of the Oz books wear out without replacing them. "This is not banning," he insisted, "it is selection."

On the local front, book lovers pressed ahead, attacking Ulveling, defending and promoting a university press publication that had now become an event of more than local interest. The *Detroit News* began serializing the classic with a daily explanation of the controversy. On April 11, Martin Gardner took the battle into the pages of the *Saturday Review* with an article entitled "The Librarians of Oz." After flushing out some more anti-Oz quoted from Florida librarians, Gardner compared them to the Wizard's Professor H. M. Wogglebug, T. E., the pompous bug whose initials stood for "Highly Magnified" and "Thoroughly Educated." On April 26 the Michigan State University *State News* got another quote from Ulveling who, in retreat, now denied banning the book on moral grounds. "We don't carry the book," he said, "because it is poorly written." The student journalists, acknowledging their newly acquired "comm skills" vocabulary, dismissed the new attack as "glittering generalities."

Lyle Blair, who had a real talent for the orchestration of outrage, responded with more comments on April 27. The *Washington Post* printed his remarks about the insatiable appetites of censors. "At first they want to censor sex and keep young minds pure, but soon they move to politics, religion and other controversial areas." Blair's eight-year-old son, David, began a week long "read-in" for fifteen children at the Campus Bookstore. On June 2 Harvey Breit of the *New York Times* quoted the Blair boy's characterization of priggish librarians as "psychoceramic," a splendid term that accurately suggested the rigid mind set of those who would ban the Wizard.

# Introduction

Whether it was a publicity stunt or a spontaneous eruption of honest outrage (and it was probably a bit of both) the tempest in the East Lansing tea cup had clearly overflowed into the national media. As interest in the Oz books intensified, the author's son, Frank Baum, Jr., responded with a letter to Ulveling and a carbon to Lyle Blair. The younger Baum demanded that Ulveling "back up your views with solid and valid facts." Baum's postscript was a sharp reminder that the library banning was a financial blessing: "you realize, of course, that the fact that the Oz books are not available in your library means a greater sale of the books at the bookstore."

To review the Great Wizard war in 1994 is to observe the special spirit of the 1950s. The Wizard war, sometimes silly, but in context, never insignificant, was an obviously minor skirmish in the larger battle to resist the anti-intellectualism and conformity of the day. By 1957 the nation had been traumatized by self-appointed snoops and heresy hunters. The term "politically correct" had not yet been coined, but the thought police had made themselves felt across the land. There were, it should be remembered, some real victims in the 1950s. Senator Joseph McCarthy's minions, Roy Cohn and G. David Schine, had stormed their way across Europe investigating "subversive" books in the U.S. Information Service libraries. In 1956 the San Francisco police had raided Lawrence Ferlinghetti's City Lights bookstore and seized copies of Allen Ginsberg's new poem *Howl*. Academic communities were not immune to the national epidemic of fear and suspicion, but Michigan State University, led by John Hannah, the first chairman of the Civil Rights Commission, was not so easily intimidated. The hapless librarian, Ralph Ulveling, and the forces he seemed to represent, were easily routed by the most lethal of weapons, laughter.

The heroes of the literary battle for the hearts and minds of children were two scholars who were able to breath new life into a neglected, almost underground, kiddie classic, an aggressive university press director who saw—and shrewdly exploited—the national implications of the conflict, and many "common" readers who viewed an attack on the Wizard as an attack on their own most cherished values.

In retrospect, we can see the Great Wizard war as a small fragment of the future. Embedded in this event were some seeds that would bloom in the following decades. The battle over books would continue with undiminished intensity. Young David Blair's "read-in" would be followed by "teach-ins" on campus when students mobilized against a real war in Vietnam. Russel Nye's once unfashionable interest in popular culture would find its fullest, almost encyclopedic, expression in 1970 when he published the highly acclaimed *The Unembarrassed Muse: The Popular Arts in America*. In 1990 another Pulitzer prize winner, the novelist Alison Lurie, would praise *The Wizard of Oz* in her *Don't Tell the Grown Ups: Subversive Children's Literature*. Lurie's book reaffirmed what those veterans of the Wizard war knew in 1957; the subversive quality of children's literature should be valued, defended, and, indeed, celebrated.

Maurice Hungiville

# WHO HE WAS

# An Appreciation

## Russel B. Nye

Y EARS from now," the New York *Times* predicted in 1919 at the death of Lyman Frank Baum, "though the children cannot clamor for the newest Oz book, the crowding generations will plead for the old ones." More than a half century after Dorothy, the Wizard, and their friends were introduced to the public, their continuing popularity testifies to the accuracy of the *Times'* estimate of Baum's work. The Land of Oz has stood the test of time.

At the age of ten, so the story goes, L. Frank Baum was fascinated by the tales of the Brothers Grimm and Hans Christian Andersen, and a trifle repelled too by their undercurrents of violence and sadness. As an adult writer of children's stories, remembering his reactions as a child, he determined to construct tales of fantasy with a difference, tales that would "bear the stamp of our times and depict the progressive fairies of today." There would be in them, he said, "no love and marriage," no hate, no revenge, no attempt to intrude into a child's world the emotions of an adult society that a child could neither experience or comprehend. He would write *American* fairy tales, using American backgrounds and materials rather than those of the European tradition familiarized by the Grimms, Perrault, Aesop, and others. In his tales, Baum wrote in the preface to *The Wizard of Oz,* "The stereotyped genie, dwarf, and fairy are eliminated, together with all the horrible and bloodcurdling incident. . . ." His were to be "modernized" fairy stories, "in which the wonderment and joy are retained, and the heartaches and nightmares left out."

· 1 ·

"Modern education," he wrote, "includes morality; therefore the modern child seeks only entertainment in its wonder-tales." His stories would be stripped of "fearsome" morality at least, and aimed simply to "excite laughter and gladden the heart."

Fortunately for three generations of children, Baum never fully succeeded in attaining all of his objectives. He drew freely on the past, and his books are far more derivative than possibly he realized. The Oz books conform to the accepted pattern far more often than they deviate. Elves, gnomes, wizards, beasts, dragons, princesses, witches, sorcery, all the conventional machinery of ancient folk and fairy tale appears in Oz, with Baum's own clever twists and adaptations. His strength as a storyteller for children lay in his unique ability to implement and adapt the familiar apparatus of the older tale by reworking old materials into new forms. He worked within the framework of the Grimm tradition despite his disavowal of many of its elements, constructing out of essentially traditional materials a fresh new gallery of characters and a group of delightfully varied plots. The changes he rang on the traditional fairy story, not his rejection of that tradition, account to a great extent for his effectiveness. A great part of the perennial attraction of the Oz books lies in the child's recognition of old friends in new roles and costumes.

The "horrible and bloodcurdling incident" to which Baum objected in the Grimms, of course, appears nowhere in Oz. Here Baum followed out his original intentions. There are excitement and danger in his stories, but violence is absent and evil under control. The witches may enchant Dorothy; they never threaten to eat her or bake her in an oven, and the bad wizards and witches who threaten Oz are frustrated creatures whom one could never imagine victorious. The Nome King, though obviously a thorough villain, is given to temper tantrums and capricious mischief much like a spoiled child, but no more dangerous and almost as easily disciplined. The Wicked Witch is defeated by a stout heart and a pail of water. The Hungry Tiger wants to eat a fat baby but his love for children won't let him—thus Baum tenderizes the tigers of folklore. Missing too are the "heartaches" of the Tin Soldier and Thumbelina, the bittersweet sentiment of Andersen,

# An Appreciation

for Oz is a land of laughter, not tears, as Baum intended it to be.

In his effort to create an American *genre*, Baum had least success and more or less gave up the attempt. The tremendous popularity of *The Wizard* surprised him. He had held really higher hopes for his next book, *Baum's American Fairy Tales: Stories of Astonishing Adventures of Boys and Girls with the Fairies of their Native Land,* which appeared in 1901. These "American" tales, laid in American locales, were lost in the instant popularity of the Oz stories, and Baum's attempt to create a native *genre* simply did not come off. Clever, inventive, with a substratum of very shrewd satire, the stories fail to measure up to the standard set by the Wizard and his crew. Nor could Baum quite keep Oz out of the book; the most effective stories in the collection are those dealing with the kingdom of Quok (another version of some of the wildly wonderful realms of the later Oz books) and with the doings of the Ryls (blood brothers of Munchkins and Gillikins).

The *American Fairy Tales* were good stories, far better than most run-of-the-mill "educational" tales for children, but in the majority of them Baum failed to observe the first rule of the wonder-tale—that it must create a never-never land in which all laws of probability may be credibly contravened or suspended. When in the first story the little girl (Dorothy by another name) replies to a puzzled, lost genie, "You are on Prairie Avenue in Chicago," the heart goes out of the story. It is only in Quok, or in Baum's zany version of the African Congo, or among the Ryls, that the book captures the fine free spirit of Oz. The child could see Chicago (or a city much like it) with his eyes; Oz he could see much more distinctly and believably with his imagination. Baum nevertheless clung for a few years to the belief that he could make the United States an authentic fairyland. "There's lots of magic in all nature," he remarked in *Tik-Tok of Oz,* "and you may see it as well in the United States, where you and I once lived, as you can here." But children could not. They saw magic only in Oz, which never was nor could be Chicago or Omaha or California or Kansas.

To everybody's good fortune, Baum gave up his idea of Americanizing Oz. What he had in mind, in effect, violated the basic laws of fantasy, and the Land of Oz could never have existed in defiance of them. The wonder-tale, to be successful, must assert the leadership of mind, establishing control over the novel and the strange, making order out of the new and disordered. It must appeal to the sense of wonder—that is, it must perceive and construct something which exists outside the immediate connotations of the materials at hand. Thus a child, given a few blocks, may see in and build from them a steam-shovel that will do all that a real steam-shovel may do and more. And the tale must contain, within a believable framework, the unbelievable elements of incantation and the supernatural, whereby all the rules of a child's world are nullified or suspended and by which the new and illogical may be selected, coordinated, and ordered. All these necessary elements appear in Oz. They could never appear in Chicago or Boston.

The Oz books became classics, then, not because Baum succeeded in writing a new kind of Americanized fairy story, but because he adapted the fairy tale tradition itself to twentieth-century American taste with imaginative ingenuity. There are in the Oz books a number of references to American locale, and Dorothy herself, of course, comes to Oz via a prairie twister. But beyond such casual references Oz has no real relation to the United States—it is fundamentally the out-of-time, out-of-space fairyland of tradition. Working from the midst of older materials, Baum's clever and occasionally brilliant variations on traditional themes are marks of craftsmanship and creativeness of a high order. It is not solely in their "Americanism," nor in their avoidance of the "horrible and bloodcurdling," nor in their rejection of moralism (which Baum did not wholly reject), nor in their pure entertainment value (which Baum did maintain), that the power of the Oz books lies. It stems rather from Baum's success in placing his work directly in the stream of the past, in his assimilation into Oz of the ageless universals of wonder and fantasy. What Baum did was to enlarge the resources of the European inheritance by making it possible to find the old joy of wonderment in the fresh new setting of Oz, creating a bright new fairyland in the old tradition.

# An Appreciation

That this was no minor achievement is shown by what happened to Baum after *The Wizard* appeared. Its popularity required a second Oz story, and then a third, until Baum, having created Oz, could not escape it. *The Wizard* was apparently written with no intention of supplying a sequel; it is a complete unit, with nothing in it to anticipate a successor, much less thirteen of them. For almost ten years after its appearance he tried hopefully to avoid writing more Oz books, producing several stories for an older age group and even some novels for adults. He even tried to end the series in 1910 with *The Emerald City of Oz*, but he was driven back to Oz by the demands of his readers and, one suspects, his own unconscious inclinations. Finally, promising that "as long as you care to read them I shall try to write them," he resigned himself to at least one Oz story a year.

Whatever Baum's original disclaimer, the strain of moralism is strong in the Oz books. They are not simply pure entertainment, devoid of any lesson, for as Baum once admitted, he tried to hide "a wholesome lesson" behind the doings of his characters. The child (or adult, for that matter) who reads the Oz books for a second or third time can usually find its hiding place, and one of the pleasures of reading Baum lies in its discovery. Baum's "wholesome lesson" is particularly evident in his creation of characters whose function is fully as much didactic as dramatic. The lesson of the Woodman, the Scarecrow, and the Lion in *The Wizard of Oz* is clearly a moral one. The Tin Woodman, a kindly, compassionate creature who weeps at stepping on a beetle, wants a heart so that he may love. The Scarecrow, who laments his lack of a brain, shows shrewd common sense from the beginning. The Cowardly Lion, when the chips are down, is as brave as a lion can be, learning (a message of reassurance to any child) that to fear danger is normal but that the important thing is to have more courage than fear. Yet not until each possesses the symbol of what he wants is he confident and satisfied—something that Dorothy wisely recognizes. You have within you, Baum seems to say, the things you seek; the symbol is of no value while the virtue is. Jack Pumpkinhead is not very smart (for his brains are pumpkin-seeds), but he is loyal, lovable, and kind—a heartening message for those at the bottom of the class.

The Wizard of Oz himself is perhaps the best example of Baum's method of indirect teaching by characterization. A gentle, inoffensive little man, the Wizard's magic is strictly of the sideshow variety. He is actually a refugee from "Bailum and Barney's" circus, where he learned a few tricks. Yet fake that he is, it is he who built Emerald City, making it a utopia out of his kindheartedness and good intent. The bluster and apparatus with which he surrounds himself hide a friendly little man; what magic he is able to work with the Woodman, the Scarecrow, and the Lion derives from his ability to capitalize on some of the foolish frailties of human nature. There is something of Colonel Sellers the salesman in the Wizard, a trace of P. T. Barnum and the "sucker born every minute" philosophy, without cruelty or intent to defraud. "How can I help being a humbug," he asks plaintively, "when all these people make me do things that everybody knows can't be done?" But there is no malice in him, and for his well-intentioned humbuggery he is rewarded by learning real sorcery from Glinda. To the child the meaning of the Wizard's story comes clear. How silly it is to turn to humbuggery to get something false, when you can have the true!

Baum had, too, a well-developed sense of satire, though satire is probably too strong a term for what Baum did. He was never zealous or intense in his attitude toward people, for his aim was amusement and not criticism. "Chaff," or "banter," describes more accurately Baum's manner of poking gently at those human frailties and foibles that the child reader could observe for himself in the world about him. The Oz stories abound with examples. The Loon People, whose King is named Bal, are inflated with self-important pretense; punctured with a thorn, they collapse as conceited people always do. The Whimsies, who have tiny heads and strong bodies, wear cardboard heads of normal size to fool observers into thinking they have brains. The China Princess, fearful that a mended crack might mar her beauty, lives a lonely, isolated life, avoiding all contact with those who might chip her perfection. The Flatheads, who had no brains at all, acted just as badly after Queen Lurline gave them some—thereby proving that it takes more than brains to make life happy and peaceful.

# An Appreciation

The Foolish Owl and the Wise Donkey illustrate how false an accepted generalization can be, and the spindly Growlywogs, who are tremendously strong, show how appearances may deceive. Flutterbudgets can never be happy because they live in constant fear of what *might* happen. Only once does Baum make obvious use of current events. General Jinjur's army of girls armed with hatpins, who go to war to force men to do housework, satirizes the suffragette movement, a reference probably too sophisticated for his child readers to identify.

One of Baum's major contributions to the tradition of the fantasy tale is his recognition of the inherent wonder of the machine, his perception of the magic of *things* in themselves. In the Oz books he expanded the resources of the fairy tale to include, for the first time, the mechanical developments of the 20th century, when every child saw about him—in the automobile, the dynamo, the radio, the airplane, and the rest—the triumph of technology over distance, time, and gravity. No American child of Baum's time or after could remain unaware of the age of invention, or fail to feel the wonderment of what machines could do. The mechanical marvels of Oz fitted exactly the technological pattern of American life, its consciousness of machinery, its faith in the machine's seemingly unlimited potential. Kipling, of course, had experimented before Baum with tales of technology, but from a much more mature and sophisticated point of view. Tom Swift, the boy's version of peculiarly American Edison-Ford myth, also made machines that outstripped reality (but not by much), but Tom's creations were always presented as real, just-around-the-corner inventions, far removed from fantasy. Baum, in a burst of inspiration, moved the machine into the child's world of imagination, endowed it with life and magic, and made it the ally of all the forces of good and justice and well-being in Oz.

The machines of Oz are magician's creations, with the white magic of the sorcerer clinging to them. By transforming the talking beasts of ancient folktales into talking machines, Baum grafted twentieth-century technology to the fairy tale tradition. The useful, friendly, companionable creatures of Oz became part of the child's family life, much as the automobile was becoming integrated into contemporary American society. The Tin Woodman, or Tik-Tok the clockwork man, the glass cats, and the robots of Oz all took on lives of their own, in the time-honored fairy tale tradition, as friends and servants. At no time did Baum allow the machines of Oz to get out of control. They are always under orderly discipline; they never exceed their limitations; they act always in harmony with the desires of those who use them. Johnny Dooit, the obliging workman who can make anything out of anything in the best Yankee "whittling boy" tradition, never uses his skill to construct anything that might threaten the peace and security of Oz. Though Smith and Tinker built a mechanical giant for the Nome King, he is a rather ineffectual robot who is easily vanquished by the wisdom of the Scarecrow and the courage of the Lion. And there are in Oz certain limits beyond which technology cannot go, however skillful the technician and powerful his magic. Ku-Klip the Tinsmith, who built the Tin Woodman and the Tin Soldier, fails dismally when he tries to construct a flesh-and-blood creature, producing only the characterless Chopfyte, who is "always somebody else." And in the end, the most ingenious mechanics of all, Smith and Tinker, overreach themselves. One paints a lake so realistically that he drowns in it; the other builds a ladder to the moon and is so fascinated by the misty, unreal Moon Country that he refuses to leave it. Thus Baum comments on technological overdevelopment, which may undo the unwary in America as it does in Oz.

The Oz books are permeated by an authentic, persistent strain of humor that is one of Baum's most easily recognized characteristics. They are fundamentally "funny" books from the child's point of view, for Baum was able, as few men are, to translate himself without condescension into the child's world. He put into the Oz books his own recognition of the incongruities of human nature, accurately catching and emphasizing some of the absurdities of life. Baum was no Swift nor Twain, but he belonged in the same tradition and his wit is (on a lesser level) astonishingly subtle and ingenious. The pertinent but unexpected association of the apparently unrelated, the joy of novelty, the pleasure of recognition of the obvious in new form, the surprise at the perception of qualities previously unseen, the shift in an accustomed framework of values—all the classic elements of the humor tradition appear in the Oz books.

Baum's wit, though, is geared to the child's pace. It is wit a child can understand and appreciate, since it deals with concepts within the circle of his experience and those which are applicable to his own sphere of action. Baum's skill in evoking a humorous response from a child is real and expert; he locates quickly and unerringly those areas of incongruity and absurdity that are recognizable to a child and subject to his judgment. There are witty bits in the Oz books that children may miss the first time, but if adults can be prevented from explaining the joke (this is almost a crime in Oz) they can have the wonderful pleasure of finding it the second or third time.

The humor of Oz lies in the interaction of character and situation, in the genuinely humorous creations who get into equally humorous predicaments because they are what they are. Sometimes the humor is broad and obvious—such as the Kingdom of Utensia, populated by kitchenware, whose King Kleaver often makes cutting remarks to Captain Dip of the Spoon Brigade. Or Grandmother Grit, who spends her time knitting, or gloomy old Pessim, who expects catastrophe any moment. At other times Baum's strokes are somewhat more delicate, as with Ann Soforth, the ambitious young queen who sets out to conquer the world with sixteen generals and one private, or with Diksey the jokester, who once made such a bad joke it led to war—both witty commentaries on military motivations. The Hammer-Heads refuse to allow travelers to enter their country since they are defending something precious; later it may occur to the reader that since nobody has ever seen what they are defending, possibly nobody wants it anyway. The best illustration of all, however, is probably H. M. Woggle-Bug, T. E., a masterpiece of humorous creation. A lowly field bug with no name at all, he hid in a schoolhouse and became thoroughly educated (T. E.) by eavesdropping on the lectures of Professor Nowitall. Caught in a magic lantern lens, he was projected on the classroom screen and stepped off highly magnified (H. M.), fully qualified to be Dean of the Royal College, "the most learned and important educator in the favored land of Oz." Thus H. M. Woggle-Bug, T. E., struts his way self-importantly through various adventures, the very symbol of ostentatious erudition. All this, and much more like it, is genuine humor, touched now and then with genius.

Beyond humor, or moral lessons, or adventure, the heart of the Oz books lies in the Land of Oz itself, which, as others have pointed out, is really an American Utopia. In Emerald City, as Baum described it, there was no disease, no illness, none but accidental death and that seldom. All inhabitants worked one-half the time and played one-half, a self-enforced obedience to the rule that all work or all play makes dullness or irresponsibility. Emerald City had no poor, because there was no money and no private property—everything belonged to the Ruler, who gave each what he needed. Among the people there was free and generous exchange of goods. Each person was "given freely by his neighbors whatever he required for his use, which is as much as anyone can reasonably desire." Foodstuffs were divided equally; clothes, jewels, shoes, housing, everything was there for the asking; and if the supply ran short, the Ruler's storehouses, filled with everything to make life perfect, lay open to the public. In Emerald City man lived in complete harmony with man, for "every inhabitant of that favored country was happy and prosperous." Men lived in complete harmony with nature and technology; machines and animals moved in and out of human society easily and naturally. So perfectly balanced was the relationship between man and nature in Oz that rains came for the asking, while courteous flies moved away unswatted when politely asked to do so. The only person in Oz who cannot understand animal talk or consort with them is the Ferryman, who as punishment for cruelty to an animal long ago is thus condemned to lonely isolation from the society of Emerald City.

The First Law of Baum's Utopia of Oz, the rule that inspires its harmonious order, is Love. This theme, on which Baum played constant and subtle variations, binds all the Oz books together as a moral unit. Love in Oz is kindness, selflessness, friendliness—an inner check that makes one act decently toward human beings, animals, plants, fairies, machines, and even one's enemies. A Love Magnet hangs over the gates of the City, so magnetizing all who enter that they must love and be loved, and Princess Ozma explains her kingdom's whole reason for existence by the simple remark, "The Land of Oz is Love." From love comes order, harmony, discipline, happiness, plenty, and perfection. And with love there is always happiness, its inseparable companion, represented in Oz by Glinda, Ozma's close friend and the greatest of sorceresses. Ruler of the Red Country of the Quadlings in southern Oz, Glinda has only one aim—to make people ever more happy. It is she, when selfishness threatens or unhappiness disturbs the Land of Oz, who appears, *dea-ex-machina,* to restore harmony, free the captive Ozma, and frustrate the forces of mischief.

The foils to Ozma, Glinda, and Oz are Ruggedo, the Nome King, and his subjects of the Nome Kingdom. (Baum thought *gnome* too difficult for children to pronounce.) The Nome King is the epitome of selfishness; his campaign against Oz is motivated solely by jealousy, conceit, tyranny, and all those qualities antithetical to love. But there is no war, for Ozma simply refuses to mobilize an army against him, in obedience to the law of Oz that "No one has a right to destroy any living creature, however evil they may be, or to hurt them, or make them unhappy." In the face of Ozma's faith and love, the Nome King is powerless. Beaten and frustrated, he is banished to wander homeless through the land. Kaliko, his successor, does better, but like the Nome King he too misuses his power and needs occasionally to be straightened out. Ozma's final victory over the Nomes comes not from magic, though she too is a mighty sorceress, but from the simple power of kindness and love.

The theme of selflessness as the cardinal principle of love runs through all the Oz books, forming the thread that binds them together. In Baum's world of Oz Bad = Selfishness, Good = Selflessness, Love = Happiness, Hate = Evil and Unhappiness. Those who use power for selfish ends, are Bad, and are punished in proportion to their crime. Coo-ee-oh, the vain narcissistic Queen of the Skeezers who lacks compassion and humanity, is punished by becoming a swan, capable only of admiring forever her cold reflection in a pool. Ugu and Gwig, minor magicians who misused their gifts, come to bad ends. Blinkie, a witch who froze the heart of a princess so that she could not love, had her magic powers stripped from her. First and Foremost, ruler of the Phanfasms, ally of the Nome King and the most evil creation in Oz (he always places himself first and foremost, the ultimate in selfishness) wants more than anything else to make people unhappy. Against Glinda and Ozma he has not even the remotest chance of winning. The villains of Oz have this in common—they cannot love, nor can they find or create happiness for themselves, even in trying to destroy it for others.

Oz is a family-style Utopia, phrased in terms and placed in a framework the child can understand. It is simply the perfect home, built on love, permeated by happiness, filled with a big loving family. In Oz you do enjoyable duties, live in cooperation and affection with brothers, sisters, neighbor children, and pets, find your wants satisfied from the storehouse of one's parents, and play in the happy security and harmony of the ideal home, where, as Baum remarks of Emerald City, "each one is proud to do all he could for his friends and neighbors." Dolls, dogs, cats, sawhorses, scarecrows, jack-o-lanterns, rugs, scissors, balloons, china dolls, and everything else in the house is alive, helpful, friendly, and full of fun. Ozma, the mother, rules with beneficence and justice. "The people were her children," Baum remarked of Ozma, "and she cared for them." Beyond the neighborhood lie thrillingly unknown lands of adventure in another part of town, where things and people may be bad or good, but always strange and exciting. If selfishness and unhappiness threaten to intrude on the serenity of family life, the toys and animals become allies and protectors, with Big Sister Glinda and Mother Ozma there to help. Oz is a fairyland small-town or suburban home, tailored to the pattern of a little girl's dream.

For Oz is beyond all doubt a little girl's dream-home. Its atmosphere is feminine, not masculine, with very little of the rowdy, frenetic energy of boys. There is no consistent father-image in Oz, or brother-image, to correspond to Ozma and Glinda. Dorothy brings Aunt Em and Uncle Henry from Kansas to Oz after her fourth trip, but they are merely the kindly farm relatives every little girl desires. Nowhere in Oz does Father appear. (It remained for Ruth Plumly Thompson, Baum's successor, to take a fall out of Father. In *The Hungry Tiger of Oz* she makes Dad the cold and distant King of Down Town, a wretched place where the single rule is "Make Money.") The Land of Oz, where Dorothy is a Princess in her own right, is all that a girl could ask for in a dream home, just as Dorothy is Baum's picture of the daughter he never had. A coolly levelheaded child in whom a refreshing sense of wonder is nicely balanced by healthy common sense, there is is nothing fey or magic about her, nothing of the storybook princess. A solid, human, child, Dorothy takes her adventure where she finds it, her reactions always generous, reasonable, and direct.

The few boys in Oz are girls' boys, drawn as little girls assume boys should be. Baum could not make Oz fit boys, nor was he capable of making boys who could fit easily and naturally into Oz society. There are no Huck Finns or Tom Sawyers in Oz, but rather a somewhat bloodless group of younger Prince Charmings. Inga, Prince of Pingaree, and Ojo, the disguised boy-prince, are little more than stuffed reproductions of traditional fairy princes. Pon, the ragged gardener's son who rises to the throne of Jinxland like an Alger hero, is not very convincing. King Bud of Noland, a merry, happy youngster, is somewhat better, though still somewhat reminiscent of a male Bobbsey twin. Zeb Hugson, Dorothy's California cousin who dropped into Oz with her in the San Francisco earthquake, is brave, kind, courteous, cheerful, and obedient, like a girl's concept of an Eagle Scout brother— but Zeb prefers his California ranch and never returns to Oz. Kiki Aru, Zeb's foil, is the prototype of the devilish younger brother. A very bad, selfish, and irritating lad, Kiki works with the Nome King to create a great deal of mischief in Oz. Cured by drinking of the Fountain of Forgetfulness (whose location many harassed sisters must have longed to find) he eventually becomes a normal boy and disappears from the story as of no further interest.

Surprisingly enough, despite the tremendous sale of Oz books during Baum's lifetime and after, neither he nor Oz received more than casual mention in contemporary surveys of children's literature, of which there were dozens published in the magazines at Christmas time. From 1900 to 1919, the years during which Baum was producing almost a book a year to the plaudits of children in the hundreds of thousands, none of his books received a review in a major journal. The lists of children's books recommended by the critics during Baum's lifetime revealed a deadly sameness—Grimm's *Fairy Tales,* Andersen, Dickens, Louisa May Alcott, Andrew Lang, Lamb's *Tales from Shakespeare,* Frances Hodgson Burnett, Miss Mulock—with an occasional daring venture into Henty, Howard Pyle, and Kenneth Grahame, or *Peter Rabbit* and *Old Mother Westwind* for the youngest.

Part of the answer lies, no doubt, in the fact that Baum set his sights (by adult critical standards) fairly low, aiming at a maximum of enjoyment with a minimum of admonition. The Oz books provided only a sketchy pattern for behavior, and in comparison to Little Lord Fauntleroy, for example, gave parents very little help in their job of adjusting and civilizing the young. This lack of overt moralizing bothered the educators and the critics of Baum's time. Hamilton Mabie, writing in *The Ladies' Home Journal* in 1907, remarked augustly, "The selection of books for childrens' reading is quite as important as the selection of food for their sustenance, but it is a duty very generally disregarded." He then proceeded to select the "best" children's books, filled with moralistic vitamins and proteins, with Baum's name conspicuously absent.

Modern critical studies of children's literature still maintain silence concerning the Oz books. The most recent and definitive study, *A Critical History of Children's Literature,* contains no mention of Baum. Entries on juvenile literature in the leading encyclopedias fail to list his name. No magazine article on Baum has ever appeared, with the exception of a short piece by James Thurber nearly twenty years ago. *Twentieth Century Authors* contains a short, inaccurate biography of Baum which includes this estimate: "The [Oz] books were lacking in style and imaginative distinction." In general, modern critics of children's literature, while admitting the appeal of the Oz books, tend to class them as popular but not worth bothering about.

It is true that the Oz books do not have the depth of Howard Pyle's re-tellings of the Robin Hood and King Arthur stories, or Kipling's Jungle Books, or the books of Kenneth Grahame or A. A. Milne. Baum's work, in the opinion of the critics, lacks literary quality. He tells his stories simply and directly, contributing little to the child's sense of language or to his awareness of its potentialities; they do not read aloud well, except with the youngest, for Baum is in no sense a stylist. There is in the Oz stories no more than a trace of fun with ideas nor any of the multi-levelled nonsense of Lear and the logical lunacy of Lewis Carroll. And there are, however much one enjoys Baum, occasional dead spots in the action of some of the later stories.

Yet one suspects, after attempting to read Carroll or Lear to a modern American child, that Baum knew better than his critics what children enjoy and understand. The nightmarish episodes, the complex paradoxes, and the logical and mathematical implications of the *Alice* books neither fit nor satisfy the child's needs and desires, however attractive they may be to mature readers. The cloying sentimentality and obsolescent vocabulary (what child of today can identify *treacle* or a *match girl?*) of many of the nineteenth century juvenile classics simply puzzle a modern youngster and leave him cold. The Wonderful Land of Oz, by contrast, is as real to him as his own neighborhood; the Scarecrow, the Woodman, and the Lion are old storybook acquaintances in new dress, familiar, friendly, and vividly alive.

It is manifestly unfair to Baum to criticize his work for its lack of those qualities, desirable as they may seem to adults, found in the great British writers of children's books. The votes of a million children who have read his books with fascination and enjoyment should most certainly be counted in the verdict. The Oz stories, as the critics must admit, fulfill all that a child may ask of a story—they are exciting, humorous, filled with fresh invention and swift action, sustained throughout by imaginativeness of a high order. Though he may have failed to create a specifically American fairyland quite as he wished, Baum's books have an indigenous flavor, reflecting American attitudes and ideals with as much accuracy and validity as the English classics reflected England's. The virtues of Oz are the homely American virtues of family love, friendliness for the stranger, sympathy for the underdog, practicality and common sense in facing life, reliance on one's self for solutions to one's problems. Dorothy, in the midst of strange and disconcerting events, retains a natural, direct approach that has an authentic American ring. No one has ever tried to interview the Wizard of Oz; Dorothy does, and neatly punctures the whole illusion. Throughout the Oz books the "good" characters maintain their self-integrity, finding their answers within themselves—an echo, perhaps of the Franklin tradition of self-help. There is no whisper of class consciousness in Oz (as there is in Alice's Wonderland) or any of the overtones of snobbery that nineteenth century juvenile fiction sometimes had. The whimsicality of the British that balances on the edge of preciousness (as in A. A. Milne) is not present in Baum, nor is the insipidity of the Milne imitators. The Oz books do have their subtleties, but the whimsy is broad and the caprice is brushed in sweeping strokes.

Baum's work does not deserve the critical neglect with which it is still treated. He wrote American tales for twentieth-century American children in an American vein, and by this he should be judged. He had his weaknesses (some of them the result of fourteen Oz books), but he had his undeniable strengths. No one can accuse him of failure to provide full measure of plot, character, and action. His plots are usually exciting, humorous, imaginative, and highly inventive. The feeling of active peril and its inevitable resolution, so essential to successful children's stories, appears in all the Oz stories as Baum sensed they must; Oz is a land of persistent danger (though not very dangerous danger) in exactly the proper degree. The perils produce no nightmares, the injustices bring no tears. The solutions satisfy the child's sense of right and justice, for Baum knew that justice put aright was the clearest principle of the child's creed and the deepest into morality that the child's tale may safely go.

In the creation of character Baum displayed his greatest mastery. Here he need bow to no one. The Tin Woodman, the Scarecrow, and the Cowardly Lion, among others, have long since secured permanent places in the gallery of great creations, and are as well known to American children as Mother Goose and Reynard the Fox. After fifty years the Land of Oz is still familiar territory; its population still provides friends and playmates for millions of children. Baum could enter into the child's world on the child's terms, create and preserve its delightful atmosphere, and tell his story with the genuine sincerity of a believer. (What child can resist an attempt to pronounce Bini Aru's unpronounceable magic word, PYRZQXGL, just to see what might happen if he *did* succeed in pronouncing it correctly? Things like this are tributes to Baum's real genius for creating belief.) Baum had the child's heart, and the child's love of the strange and beautiful and good, with the ability to bring them all alive. For this gift he deserves recognition.

# The Royal Historian of Oz

## MARTIN GARDNER

*"It is not down on any map; true places never are."*
—MELVILLE

AMERICA'S greatest writer of children's fantasy was, as everyone knows except librarians and critics of juvenile literature, L. Frank Baum. His *Wonderful Wizard of Oz* has long been the nation's best known, best loved native fairy tale, but you will look in vain for any recognition of this fact in recent histories of children's books. Aside from an obscure booklet by Edward Wagenknecht and a brief magazine article by James Thurber, no one has felt it worth while to inquire as to what merits the Oz books may have or what manner of man it was who first produced them. By and large, the critics have looked upon Baum's efforts as tawdry popular writing in a class with Tom Swift and Elsie Dinsmore; certainly not to be compared with such classic "children's" fantasies as *Pilgrim's Progress* or *Gulliver's Travels*.

Fortunately, children themselves seldom listen to such learned opinion. Nothing in the world could induce them to plod their way through Bunyan's dreary discourse on Protestant fundamentalism or Swift's impudent nose-thumbing at the human race. Even Lewis Carroll's Alice books, with their archaic British phrases, abrupt transitions and nightmarish episodes, have lost almost all their appeal for a modern child unless he happens to be a prodigy who plays chess and dabbles in semantics and symbolic logic. Yet today, half a century after they were written, children still turn the pages of Baum's Oz books with passionate delight. Surely it is only a matter of time until the critics develop sufficient curiosity to read the books themselves. When they do they will be startled to find them well written, rich in excitement, humor, and philosophy, and with sustained imaginative invention of the highest order. In anticipation, therefore, of this event, it may be of interest to recount here for the first time the full story of Baum's remarkable career.

Lyman Frank Baum was born May 15, 1856, in the little town of Chittenango, near Syracuse, N. Y. His mother, Cynthia Stanton, was Scotch-Irish in descent and a devout Episcopalian. On his father's side his ancestors came from Germany, settling in Central New York in 1748. His grandfather, the Rev. John Baum, was a circuit-riding Methodist minister. Benjamin Ward Baum, his father, was one of the nation's earliest oil producers, with extensive holdings in the Pennsylvania oil fields, and owner of a large estate near Syracuse in an area that is now the town of Mattydale.

Baum's childhood was spent in comparative luxury at Rose Lawn, the name of his father's estate. Here he was privately tutored except for a short period of attendance at Peekskill Military Academy. Young Frank did not take to military discipline, a fact that may explain the satire that pervades his descriptions of the Royal Army of Oz. (For a time it numbered 27 officers and one private named Omby Amby, though on most occasions it consisted only of the Soldier with the Green Whiskers.)

When Baum was entering his teens, his father bought him a small printing press. For several years, during the summer months, Frank and his younger brother Harry wrote and printed a monthly newspaper that they called the *Rose Lawn Home Journal.* This may have aroused Frank's interest in a newspaper career. At any rate, at the age of seventeen he took a job in Manhattan as cub reporter on the *New York World.* Two years later we find him opening his own printing shop at Bradford, Pa., where he established the *New Era,* a paper still published today. But the work was dull and his spirit restless. For a while he managed a small chain of "opera houses" owned by his father in New York and Pennsylvania.

The theatrical world fascinated him more and more. Occasionally he acted with traveling stock companies, using a stage name because his family frowned on his associations with the theater. At one time he even tried to make a go of his own Shakespearean troupe. Finally he turned to play writing and in 1881 achieved his first literary success with an Irish musical comedy called *The Maid of Arran*. The play opened at his own opera house in Gilmour, Pa., then moved to Manhattan where it enjoyed a profitable run. Baum wrote the book, music, and lyrics, produced and directed, and under the name of Louis F. Baum, played the romantic lead! His acting was described in one review as "quiet and effective."[1]

Judging by early descriptions, young Baum must have made an impressive stage appearance. He was slightly over six feet, slender and athletically proportioned, with brown hair, gray eyes, fair skin, and handsome angular features. His voice was low and well modulated and he sang in a rich baritone. In later years he always wore a large bicycle-handle mustache that was fashionable in his time. In photographs his eyes seem humorous, kindly, dreamy.

During the first year of his play's success, Baum married Maud Gage, of Fayetteville, N. Y., an attractive, spirited girl whose strong will and practical mind served to counter-balance her husband's reluctance to take money matters seriously. It proved to be a permanent, happy marriage. The play was on the road for several years, but when Maud became pregnant, Baum dropped out of the cast and returned with her to Syracuse. There he set up a small company to manufacture and sell "Baum's Castorine," a crude oil product used for greasing axles. This aspect of the oil business did not long hold his interest. He tried his hand at three more Irish melodramas—*Matches, Kilmourne,* and *The Queen of Killarney*. Only the first two were actually produced. They enjoyed brief runs but failed to achieve the popularity of his first play.

In 1887, with two small sons to support, Baum turned his face westward in search of greener pastures. His wife had a brother living in Aberdeen, a small prairie town in the region that was soon to become the State of South Dakota, and it was there that Baum took his family. At first he ran a variety store called Baum's Bazaar, but his generosity with credit made it difficult to keep the business solvent. He next bought a weekly paper, the *Aber-*

*deen Saturday Pioneer,* and edited it for two years. "Our Land-lady," his front page column, poked good-natured fun at the local gentry but apparently made a few enemies. There were later rumors that he became involved in a pistol duel with one villager. The duel began with the two men standing back to back in the middle of the street. They were instructed to walk away from each other to the ends of the block, circle the block, and start shooting as they came together on the opposite side. Each man, as soon as he turned his first corner, reportedly ran up an alley and vanished from the scene.[2]

Two more sons were born in Aberdeen. The paper failed in 1891 and Baum moved his family to Chicago where he first took a job as reporter on the *Chicago Post.* For a time he traveled through the Middle West selling china and glassware for a Chicago importing firm while his wife supplemented the family income by doing embroidery. His luck turned in 1897 when he tapped a hitherto unexploited magazine field by founding the *Show Window,* a monthly periodical for window trimmers. It was the official organ of the National Association of Window Trimmers of America of which Baum was founder and first president.

For some time Baum had delighted his four sons by telling them ingenious tales that amplified the meaning of familiar Mother Goose rhymes. He began putting these stories on paper and in 1897 a collection was published by the Chicago firm of Way and Williams in a handsome format with illustrations by Maxfield Parrish. *Mother Goose in Prose,* as it was called, was Baum's first book for children as well as Parrish's first job of book illus-trating.[3] It must have sold well because it soon appeared in a London printing and in several other American editions.

Baum's next book, *By the Candelabra's Glare,* is now extremely rare and much sought by collectors. He issued it himself in 1898, setting the type, printing, and even binding it in his own work-shop. It is a collection of sentimental, undistinguished verse. "My best friends have never called me a poet," he confesses in the foreword, "and I have been forced to admire their restraint." One poem, "La Reine Est Morte— Vive la Reine!", is an amusing attack on the type of woman then active in the Feminist movement. The third stanza reads:

> And shout hurrah for the woman
> new!
> With her necktie, shirt and tooth-
> pick shoe,
> With tailor-made suit and mien
> severe
>
> She's here!

Baum's mother-in-law was a prominent feminist, a fact that may help explain his dislike of the New Woman. Even the Oz books contain many sly digs at the suffragettes, and one book, *The Land of Oz*, is one long satire on the movement. It chronicles the temporary overthrow of Oz by an army of comely young women.[4] The Revolution is bloodless, owing to the fact that the Royal Army (*i.e.*, the Soldier with the Green Whiskers) flees in terror when the girls brandish their knitting needles at him. Once the female dictatorship is established, the husbands of Oz are forced to take over all the former duties of their wives. This proves annoying to both wives and husbands, but luckily the throne is soon restored.

General Jinjur, the pretty farm girl who leads the revolt, is one of Baum's best "meat people" characterizations (in Oz "meat people" are sharply distinguished from such personages as the Scarecrow and Tin Woodman who have no flesh and blood). She is a shrewdly drawn portrait of the masculine protest type. Her face wears "an expression of discontent coupled to a shade of defiance or audacity." She walks with "swift strides" and there is about her "an air of decision and importance." In a later Oz book she blacks her husband's eye for milking a red cow when she wanted him to milk the white one. Whenever the Scarecrow's painted face becomes faded, it is Jinjur who enjoys retouching it. It is not her own face that she paints, but that of a straw man.

Baum's third hard-cover work, published in 1899, was *Father Goose, His Book*. It is a collection of nonsense rhymes for children, illustrated by Baum's friend William Wallace ("Den") Denslow, a Chicago newspaper artist, and hand-lettered by another Chicago artist and friend, Ralph Fletcher Seymour.[5] To everyone's surprise the book was an immediate sell-out, requiring four re-printings in the three months that followed the first edition.

For several years Baum had been taking his family each sum-mer to Macatawa, a Michigan resort town on the shore of Lake Michigan. With the money earned by *Father Goose* he had a sum-mer cottage built there which he named "The Sign of the Goose." Most of the furniture was built by Baum himself. Since early manhood he had suffered from a bad heart and his doctor had advised him to do more of the manual craft work that he so much enjoyed. It was characteristic of Baum that he used the goose as the decorative motif of his cottage. A large rocking chair was in the shape of a goose. A frieze of green geese bordered the living room walls. A stained glass window portrayed a goose in brilliant colors. Even the tiny brass heads of his upholstery tacks were specially made for him in the shape of geese![6]

Baum continued to edit his trade journal and in 1900 published *The Art of Decorating*, a mammoth handbook on the decoration of store windows and interiors. But his interest had now shifted to juvenile writing and his head was brimming with unusual ideas. During that year four children's books came from his pen. Two were unimpressive—*The Army Alphabet* and *The Navy Alphabet,* oversize books of mediocre verse telling the reader that A stands for Admiral, B for Bulwark, and so on. The other two books were fantasies, each concerned with adventures in a mythi-cal land of enchantment. *A New Wonderland* had as its setting the Beautiful Valley of Phunnyland where it snows popcorn, rains lemonade, and "the thunder is usually a chorus from the opera of Tannhauser." The other book—the book destined to make him immortal—was *The Wonderful Wizard of Oz.*

*A New Wonderland* (later retitled *The Magical Monarch of Mo)* is a collection of short, hilarious tales. It was written for an eastern firm and published by them at about the same time that *The Wonderful Wizard of Oz* was issued by George M. Hill, the small Chicago House that had published *Father Goose. The Wonderful Wizard* almost failed to find a publisher. It was turned down by every house to which it was submitted, Mrs. Baum later recalled in a letter,[7] because it was "too different, too radical—out of the general line." Mr. Hill finally consented to act as the book's distributor only after Baum and his illustrator, Denslow, agreed to shoulder all printing expenses. The book was not actually distributed to stores until the fall, but before the end of the year it had become the fastest selling children's book in America. In 1955 a first edition sold at auction in Manhattan for six hundred dollars.

The book's story, as everyone knows, is about a plain-spoken little orphan girl who suddenly finds herself, like Lewis Carroll's Alice, in a magic land. Alice fell into Wonderland by way of a rabbit hole. Dorothy Gale is blown into Oz by a Kansas cyclone. And behind her strange adventures, as in all of Baum's fantasies, there lurks many an intended level of higher meaning. The Cowardly Lion, Scarecrow, and Tin Woodman illustrate delightfully the human tendency to confuse a real virtue with its valueless outer symbols. The Lion wants the Wizard to give him courage, the Scarecrow wants brains, and the Tin Woodman desires, beneath the coldness of his metal exterior, a warm heart. All three possess, of course, the things they seek. The Lion quakes with fear but meets all danger bravely. The Scarecrow thinks better than anyone in the party, and the Tin Woodman is so concerned over his lack of heart that his "Reverence for Life" exceeds that of a Schweitzer. On one occasion when he accidentally steps on a beetle he weeps so copiously that his tears rust and lock his jaws.

Even the ancient philosophic question of which is superior, the head or the heart, is explicitly raised. "I shall ask for brains instead of a heart," remarks the straw man, "for a fool would not know what to do with a heart if he had one." To which the tin man replies, "I shall take the heart, for brains do not make one happy, and happiness is the best thing in the world."

Baum wisely adds: "Dorothy did not say anything, for she was puzzled to know which of her two friends was right."

After the success of *The Wonderful Wizard,* Baum handed his trade journal over to a new editor and began work in earnest on other books for children. Three were published in 1901, none about Oz. *Dot and Tot of Merryland* is a full length fantasy for very young readers. *The Master Key,* for older boys, is a science fiction story about the wonders of electricity. The third volume, *Baum's American Fairy Tales,* deserves special mention because it marks the first appearance in American letters of fairy tales of merit that have the United States as a setting.

In 1902 Baum published *The Life and Adventures of Santa Claus,* a warm, moving story told in almost Biblical prose and involving an elaborate Dunsany-like mythology. Its appearance, however, was completely overshadowed by the success in Chicago of a musical extravaganza based on *The Wizard.* Baum wrote both book and lyrics, Paul Tietjens composed the music, and Denslow designed the costumes.[8] The original script was so heavily revised by Julian Mitchell, the producer, that it bore little resemblance to the original. Oz fans are usually shocked to learn that in the stage version Dorothy's pet is not a little black dog named Toto, but a huge cow called Imogene. There is a Lady Lunatic, very much out of place in Oz, and even a Poet Prince with whom Dorothy falls in love!

Baum first reacted to many of these changes with amazement and indignation, but after the musical had become a smashing success, playing eighteen months on Broadway, he decided that Mitchell knew his audiences. In concluding a letter to the *Chicago Tribune* (Sunday, June 26, 1904, Part IV, p. 1) he expressed his views as follows:

"I confess, after two years of success for the extravaganza, that I now regard Mr. Mitchell's views in a different light. The people will have what pleases them, and not what the author happens to favor, and I believe that one of the reasons why Julian Mitchell is recognized as a great producer is that he faithfully tries to serve the great mass of playgoers—and usually succeeds.

"My chief business is, of course, the writing of fairy tales, but should I ever attempt another extravaganza, or dramatize another of my books, I mean to profit by the lesson Mr. Mitchell has taught me, and sacrifice personal preference to the demands of those I shall expect to purchase admission tickets."

# The Royal Historian of Oz

Two vaudeville comedians who worked as a team, Fred Stone and Dave Montgomery, were catapulted to stardom by the stage success of *The Wizard*. Stone played the Scarecrow and Montgomery the Tin Woodman. (The role of Dorothy, it is interesting to note, was taken by Anna Laughlin, mother of today's "star-spangled soprano," Lucy Monroe.) The two comics were in England when Mitchell wired them to return for parts in the musical. New York papers reported that Mitchell met Stone with the comment, "Fred, you are a perfect scarecrow." To which Stone indignantly replied that his clothes had been made by one of the finest tailors in England. A chapter of Fred Stone's autobiography, *Rolling Stone*, published in 1945, is devoted to the musical. It is interesting to learn from this that Fred's brother, Edwin, took the role of Dorothy's pet cow, and that Fred fell in love with and married the girl who played the Lady Lunatic.

Flushed with the success of his musical, Baum and his wife sailed for Europe in January of 1906 for a six-month vacation abroad. The trip took them through Egypt, Greece, Italy, North Africa, Switzerland, and France. Baum's heart condition prevented him from climbing to the top of the Great Pyramid, a challenge that his robust wife was unable to resist. "The steps are from three to four feet in height," Maud wrote in a letter home, "and the ascent so strenuous that I rested several times on the way up."[9] A dramatic eruption of Mt. Vesuvius, witnessed by the Baums, prompted him to write a friend that the crater was the only thing he had seen on the trip that smoked more than he did.

Paul Tietjens, who wrote *The Wizard's* musical score, also took a vacation abroad, spending it in Paris with Denslow. There he met and married the American girl who later became the poet Eunice Tietjens. In her autobiography, *The World at My Shoulder*, she describes Denslow as "a delightful old reprobate who looked like a walrus." Back in the States, she and her husband called on Baum at his Michigan cottage, "The Sign of the Goose."

"L. Frank Baum was a character," she writes. "He was tall and rangy, with an imagination and a vitality which constantly ran away with him. He never wrote fewer than four books a year. . . . Constantly exercising his imagination as he did, he had come to the place where he could honestly not tell the difference between what he had done and what he had imagined. Everything he said had to be taken with at least a half-pound of salt.[10] But he was a fascinating companion.

"He was never without a cigar in his mouth, but it was always unlit. His doctor had forbidden him to smoke, so he chewed up six cigars a day instead. There was one exception to this. Before he took his swim in the lake in the afternoon he would light a cigar and walk immediately into the water. He would solemnly wade out till the water was up to his neck and there walk parallel with the shore, moving his arms to give the impression that he was swimming. When a wave splashed on the cigar and put it out he at once came in and dressed.

"His house was full of the most remarkable mementos of the time when it had been necessary for him 'to rest his brain,' following a stroke of facial paralysis. He had painted the walls with stencilled designs; he had made a sign of wrought iron and painted wood for the dooryard, 'At the Sign of Father Goose'; he had made furniture; he had written a small book of poems (!), had set it up in type himself, printed and bound it by hand. Last of all, because all this had not yet rested his brain enough, he had made an elaborate piano arrangement of Paul's music for *The Wizard of Oz*—though he was no musician it was pretty good—had then figured out the system by which pianola records were made, and had cut a full-length record of this arrangement out of wrapping paper! This seems to have done the trick, and he was presently back at work."

Surviving friends of Baum all remember him as a modest, dignified gentleman who enjoyed meeting people, talking, and telling funny stories. "He was a very kindly man," Mrs. Baum states in a letter, "never angry, pleasant to everyone, but when his mind was active with some story he would meet his best friend and not see him."[11]

Throughout his adult life Baum did not affiliate with any church organization save for a brief period of membership in an Episcopalian church in Aberdeen. But he was always a "religious" man in the sense that he believed in both God and immortality. For a time he was intrigued by theosophy, and although he rejected most of the preposterous doctrines of this cult, he seems to have retained a belief in reincarnation and the law of Karma. His eldest son Frank, now a retired Army colonel in Los Angeles, tells me in a letter that his father always believed that he and his wife had been together in previous incarnations and would be together again in future lives. (In Baum's fantasies I can recall only two places where he touches on the question of soul survival. *Sea Fairies* has a satirical section in which a school of "holy" mackerel express their conviction that when they are jerked out of their element by a hook, they "go to glory"—to an "unknown, but beautiful sea." And in *Sky Island,* when inhabitants of the blue region reach the close of their life, they walk through the Arch of Phinis into the Great Blue Grotto, but what happens to them on the other side is not known.)

Aside from marching in a few torchlight parades for William Jennings Bryan, Baum was as inactive in politics as in church affairs. He consistently voted as a democrat, however, and his sympathies seem always to have been on the side of the laboring classes. (In *Sea Fairies* an octopus expresses great indignation at having been likened to the Standard Oil monopoly!) I do not know whether Baum ever read William James, but he certainly shared James' love of variety, and democratic tolerance for ways of life alien to his own. There is a remarkable scene in *The Lost Princess of Oz* (p. 148) in which a group of animals, meat and meatless, argue about who among them is superior. The matter is finally settled by the Cowardly Lion who says quietly:

"Were we all like the Sawhorse we would all be Sawhorses, which would be too many of the kind; were we all like Hank, we would be a herd of mules; if like Toto, we would be a pack of dogs; should we all become the shape of the Woozy, he would no longer be remarkable for his unusual appearance. Finally, were you all like me, I would consider you so common that I would not care to associate with you. To be individual, my friends, to be different from others, is the only way to become distinguished from the common herd. Let us be glad, therefore, that we differ from one another in form and in disposition. Variety is the spice of life and we are various enough to enjoy one another's society; so let us be content."

This theme of tolerance runs through all of Baum's writings, with many episodes that poke fun at narrow nationalism and ethnocentrism. In *John Dough and the Cherub,* for example, we encounter the Hilanders who are tall and thin, their country separated by a stone wall from the Lolanders who are short and fat. A law observed in both regions forbids anyone to ask questions of strangers or of inhabitants on the opposite side of the wall. As a consequence, neither country knows anything about the other, regarding its own area as a paradise and inhabitants on the other side as barbarians.

Like William Morris whom he read and admired, Baum had a constitutional dislike of the mass-produced item, whether a piece of furniture or a man. "After all," says the Scarecrow to Tommy Kwikstep (a boy with twenty legs), "you have the pleasure of knowing you are unusual, and therefore remarkable among the people of Oz. To be just like other persons is small credit to one, while to be unlike others is a mark of distinction." I can think of only one spot outside of Oz where individuals of eccentric appearance do not suffer because of their deviation from the norm, and that is in the world of the carnival and circus sideshow. Perhaps it was his circus background that enabled the Wizard to adjust so easily to life in Oz.

Eccentric as Baum's "meatless" characters are, they have a consistency of personality and behavior that makes them very real to the mind of a child. On one occasion when Baum had not written for weeks, Maud asked him what the trouble was. "They won't do what I want them to," he replied. When he began writing again and she asked how the matter had been settled, his answer was, "By letting them do what they wanted to."[12] It is a believable answer. Baum was a natural storyteller and even his most outlandish characters seem always to move about with a life of their own.

In spite of the fact that he continued to receive hundreds of letters (a mere trickle of the deluge to come!) from children who wanted to hear more about Oz, Baum's interests still lay in fairy tales of other sorts. His *Enchanted Island of Yew,* 1903, is not a bad story (the chapter on Twi, a land where everything exists in double form, is an amazing *tour de force*) but it did not sell well, and it is marred by unpleasant psychological undertones.

Finally, in 1904, Baum yielded to the persistent demands of his readers. He wrote *The Marvelous Land of Oz* (later retitled *The Land of Oz*), dedicating it to Montgomery and Stone. It is his only Oz book in which Dorothy does not appear. The central character, a small boy named Tip, is later revealed to be Princess Ozma in enchanted form. For many years the Baums had longed for a daughter, and the book's dramatic climax may well have been an expression of such a desire.

Many new and entertaining "meatless" characters are introduced in the story. Jack Pumpkinhead is an awkward wooden figure whose head is a pumpkin carved in an eternal grin. A wooden sawhorse is brought to life, much to its own astonishment. And of course we must not fail to mention Professor H. M. Woggle-Bug, T. E.

The Woggle-Bug is Baum's caricature of the over-educated pedant. He had originally been an ordinary woggle-bug, living in the hearth of a country schoolhouse. There he had become extremely learned by listening to the lectures of Professor Nowit-all. One day the professor discovered him in the room, and to show his pupils what a woggle-bug looked like, put him in a magic lantern that projected his magnified image on the screen. At a moment when the attention of the class was distracted, the woggle-bug stepped down from the screen and made an escape in his greatly puffed-up condition. "H. M." stands for "Highly Magnified," and "T. E." for "Thoroughly Educated." The Woggle-Bug is addicted to using big words and has to be rebuked occasionally for his tendency to indulge in bad puns. This is partly a satire on Baum himself, for the Oz books abound in puns. They reach a crescendo in a later book when Dorothy visits the Kingdom of Utensia where all the citizens are pieces of kitchenware. In eight pages of text Baum manages to introduce no less than fifty puns!

The Woggle-Bug eventually becomes the President of the College of Art and Athletic Perfection. His great contribution to the higher learning is the invention of a pill that gives a student all the knowledge he needs simply by swallowing it. This frees students from the burden of attending classes and permits them to spend all their time on college sports.

*The Woggle-Bug,* an operetta which Baum based on *The Land of Oz,* was produced in Chicago in 1905, but its run was short. *The Woggle-Bug Book,* issued the same year to publicize the play, is now a rare collector's item. It is a large picture book in paper covers, telling of the Woggle-Bug's adventures in an American city.

In addition to his summer home at Macatawa, Baum now began spending part of each winter in a cottage at Coronado, on the California coast. In 1905 he purchased Pedloe Island, 80 miles off the coast, and announced to the press his plans to convert the island into a miniature land of Oz that would serve as a playground for youngsters. An eleven-year old San Francisco girl was appointed Princess of Oz. A palace and statues of leading Oz personages were to be erected, and a monument to Jack Pumpkinhead built on Wizard's Point. The project never got beyond the planning stage and may have been little more than a publicity stunt to promote the sale of the second Oz book.

*Queen Zixi of Ix,* Baum's effort to write an old-fashioned European type fairy tale, appeared in 1905. That same year Baum tried his hand at an adult novel. *The Fate of a Crown,* a romantic tale about Brazil, was published under the pseudonym of Schuyler Staunton. Another romance by Staunton, *Daughters of Destiny,* came out the following year. His final attempt along these lines was *The Last Egyptian,* issued anonymously in 1908. The three novels are well written adventure tales, but otherwise have little to recommend them.

Six other pseudonyms were used by Baum. Captain Hugh Fitzgerald was his *nom de plume* for two boys' books about the adventures of one Sam Steele. Six novels about the Boy Fortune Hunters (two were reprints of the Sam Steele books) came out under the name of Floyd Akers. John Estes Cooke (not to be confused with John Esten Cooke, a Virginia historian whom Baum may have admired) was the name he used for a privately printed edition of *Tamawaca Folks.* Tamawaca is an anagram for Macatawa. The novel is about Baum's friends in the resort area.

Under the name of Edith Van Dyne, Baum wrote seventeen novels for teen age girls. Ten of them are about Aunt Jane's nieces, five about Mary Louise, and two about Orissa Kane, a girl aviator. After Baum's death, books by Edith Van Dyne continued to appear but were the product of other hands. *Annabel,* a love story about a red-haired lass, was written under the pseudonym of Suzanne Metcalf. As Laura Bancroft he published six small books of fantasy (subsequently issued as a single volume called *Twinkle and Chubbins*) and *Policeman Bluejay,* a longer fantasy (later issued as *Babes in Birdland*). With the possible exception of the Bancroft books, none of these pseudonymous works are of lasting value. But the potboilers for older boys and girls, including two published under his own name (*The Daring Twins* and *Phoebe Daring*) brought him a steady and considerable income.

On one occasion, Mrs. Baum recalls,[13] an eastern publisher visiting in Chicago expressed to Baum's publisher a strong desire to meet Mrs. Van Dyne. He was so persistent that the firm finally arranged a tea at which the visitor was introduced to a lady who had been carefully coached to play the role. The publisher was charmed and edified. Baum and his wife attended the tea, enjoying the hoax immensely.

In 1907 Baum returned to his role of Father Goose by publishing *Father Goose's Year Book,* a kind of diary with blank pages on the right and humorous poems and aphorisms (such as "Rolling billiard balls gather no salary") on the left. But Baum's readers were no longer interested in Father Goose; they wanted to hear more about Oz. The second Oz book had not concerned Dorothy —in fact no one from the "outside world" appeared in the story. But readers remembered Dorothy with fondness, and yielding to their entreaties, Baum reintroduced her as the protagonist of *Ozma of Oz,* the third volume in the series.

Dorothy's companion on this second adventure is a proud yellow hen called Billina. Other "Ozzy" characters also introduced for the first time include Tik-Tok, a mechanical copper man; the Hungry Tiger who longs to eat little babies but whose conscience never permits him to do so (the *id* versus the *super-ego!*); and the Nome King, a whimsical mixture of evil and the comic, who appears in many later Oz books as the sworn enemy of Dorothy and Ozma.

Tik-Tok is one of the earliest robots in American fantasy. As his directions for winding read, he "thinks, speaks, acts, and does everything but live." Parts of his mechanism are always running down at crucial moments. Once in a later book he lapses into double-talk when his thought mechanism, but not his speech, ceases to function.

The remaining Oz books, all excellent though some have sections of careless writing, contain scores of outrageous personages. There is the Woozy, a blue, square-shaped animal of wood whose eyes dart fire whenever anyone says "Krizzle-Kroo" (the Woozy does not understand what this means and it is this that makes him so furious). There is the Patchwork Girl, a cotton-stuffed, but far from stuffy figure whose meeting with the Scarecrow is one of the highlights of the book in which she first appears. Nor does one easily forget such minor characters as Johnny Dooit, with the long gray whiskers and copper tool chest, who can build anything in just a few seconds; the Braided Man who sells boxes of assorted ruffles for ladies' skirts and flutters for flags; the Fuddles, a race of 3-D jigsaw people who "scatter" when disturbed, thereby giving befuddled visitors the fun of putting them together again.

The two most important cats in Oz deserve a paragraph. Both behave exactly as you would expect cats to behave if they could talk. Eureka, Dorothy's meat cat, permits herself to undergo a long court trial to determine if she has eaten one of the Wizard's piglets before she informs the court where the little pig can be found. Bungles, a glass cat with a cold ruby heart, is so reluctant to show her emotions that once when she leaves to obtain help for friends in distress, she moves very slowly to give the impression she is indifferent to their fate. As soon as she is out of sight, however, she runs like a streak of crystal.

At the close of *The Emerald City of Oz,* sixth in the series,

Baum tried to drop the series altogether. Glinda, the most powerful sorceress in Oz, casts a spell over the country that makes it impossible for the Royal Historian to find out what is happening inside its borders. You can imagine, of course, the flood of letters from heartbroken youngsters! Fortunately Baum was able to reestablish communication with the Shaggy Man, by wireless, and thus continue the series. Before writing the seventh Oz book, however, he managed to finish two superbly written fantasies, *Sea Fairies* and *Sky Island*. They tell of the adventures of Mayre Griffiths, better known as Trot, and her peg-legged sailor companion, Cap'n Bill. Both Trot and Cap'n Bill later become honored citizens of Oz.

Certainly one reason for the immense popularity of the Oz books is the fact that they are told with such a wealth of detail that a strong sense of reality is created. These details range from such trifling observations as the fact that the Scarecrow has difficulty picking up small objects with his padded fingers, to important data about the history, geography, and customs of Oz. There is even a map of Oz, drawn by Professor Woggle-Bug. It formed the front end-paper of early editions of *Tik-Tok of Oz* and also was issued separately as a book insert.

No Oz reader need be told that Oz is roughly rectangular and divided into four regions, each with a characteristic color. The first edition of *The Road to Oz* was actually printed on tinted paper that changed color each time the scene shifted to another region! In the center of Oz is the Emerald City (a reflection of Baum's love of Ireland) where Princess Ozma rules in a palace of glittering gems. Surrounding Oz on all four sides is the Deadly Desert. Anyone setting foot on the desert turns instantly into a grain of sand.

Many social and economic details about Oz are known. Its population is more than half a million. The Emerald City, at the time it was almost conquered by the Nome King, had 9,654 buildings, 57,318 inhabitants. There is no sickness or disease in Oz. No one grows older and death occurs only rarely.[14] All animals talk in Oz and they are treated with as much respect as humans. In many ways Oz resembles the anarchist utopia of William Morris' *News from Nowhere.*[15] There is virtually no police force because all Ozites are happy, unselfish, and law-abiding. They work half the time, play half the time. There is no money, no rich, no poor. "Each person," the Royal Historian tells us, "was given freely by his neighbors whatever he required for his use, which is as much as anyone may reasonably desire."

Fortunately, not all parts of Oz are this orderly—especially the wild, unsettled areas of the Gillikin and Quadling regions where many queer and unruly races flourish. Otherwise there would be no dangers and consequently no adventures.

Dangers yes, but horrors no. It is a rare occasion when Baum describes a scene that might frighten a sensitive child. Only a morbid adult could object to a wicked witch melting away or Jack Pumpkinhead carving a new head for himself to replace a former one that has spoiled. Baum's intention, stated in the preface of *The Wizard,* to leave out the "heartaches and nightmares" was amply fulfilled. You have only to glance through Grimm and Andersen, *Pinocchio,* or many another classic fairy tale to realize how skillfully Baum managed in contrast with these works, to retain the excitement and avoid the violence and tears. Perrault's original story of Red Riding Hood, still the version told to French children, ends with the wolf eating both the little girl and her grandmother. I am told that youngsters in France find this highly amusing. A respectable case can even be made for the view that violent images provide a healthy purging of a child's sadistic emotions as well as a valuable early introduction to the reality of evil. "Children love a lot of nightmare and at least a little heartache in their books," writes Thurber, and he for one is glad that Baum did not succeed completely in keeping these elements out of his work.[16] It is true that Baum occasionally forgot his promise, especially in *Dorothy and the Wizard in Oz* where an atmosphere of violence and gloom hangs over a large part of the tale, and in the macabre episode (in a later book) of the Tin Woodman's conversation with his former head. But on the whole his books are singularly free of shocking scenes and the spirit of Oz is a happy, sunny one. There are only two references in all of Baum's Royal History to it having rained in Oz.

# The Royal Historian of Oz

Literary masterpieces are often written with astonishing carelessness of detail. Cervantes completely forgot that Sancho Panza's ass had been stolen; with no word of explanation we find Sancho riding him again. Robinson Crusoe strips off his clothes, swims out to the wreckage of a ship, and a moment later we find him filling his pockets with biscuits from the ship's bread room. Like the Baker Street Irregulars who delight in inventing plausible explanations for Watson's memory lapses, a group of Oz enthusiasts can spend many pleasant hours suggesting ways for harmonizing similar contradictions in the Royal History.

The Land of Ev, for example, lies just across the Deadly Desert. But in what direction? You can find a basis for placing it to the north, south, east, or west of Oz. The early history of Oz, before the Wizard arrived in his balloon, is riddled with difficulties. There is reason to believe that grass takes on the color of each region in Oz and equally good reason to think it doesn't. Exactly what happens when a Nome touches an egg? Does he wither away or turn into a mortal? Why do the Shaggy Man and Polychrome, the Rainbow's daughter, act like strangers when they meet (in *Tik-Tok of Oz*) for the second time? These are only a fraction of the tantalizing problems that face the student of Oz.

An equally fascinating pastime is to speculate on how Baum arrived at the names of various characters and countries. In many instances the basis is obvious. For example, Princess Langwidere is a haughty woman with a "languid air." General Jinjur is a girl with lots of "ginger." But what about Woot the Wanderer, protagonist of *The Tin Woodman of Oz?* Did Baum take the initials of the tin man's title then switch the "T" from front to back?

The word Oz itself has been the subject of much speculation. The most popular theory is that Baum, searching for a name, looked up at a filing cabinet and saw the words "From O to Z." Another is that it came from "Boz," the nickname of Charles Dickens, one of Baum's favorite authors. And someone has pointed out that Job lived in the land of Uz. The late Jack Snow advanced a captivating theory in the preface of his monumental *Who's Who in Oz*. Baum once wrote that he had always enjoyed stories that cause the reader to exclaim with "Ohs" and "Ahs" of wonder, and

Mr. Snow points out that Oz can be pronounced either "Ohs" or "Ahs."

The Baums moved to Los Angeles in 1909. Baum constructed an enormous circular birdcage in the garden of his home and stocked it with a large variety of song birds. This love of wildlife is reflected in all of Baum's writings, and one has the feeling that when the Tin Woodman expresses horror at the thought of injuring a butterfly, he is expressing the sentiments of the author. Baum never cared for hunting and fishing. In early life his favorite outdoor sports seem to have been swimming, archery, and motor boating, though as he approached his sixties he turned more to golf and gardening. When the Baums moved to Hollywood in 1910, a large garden surrounded Ozcot, Baum's name for the house he built there. Baum won many cups in state flower competitions and even became known locally as "The Chrysanthemum King of Southern California."

At the time Ozcot was built, Hollywood was still a small suburban town. The infant movie industry then centered in New York. But as Jack Snow has observed, Baum was unable to escape from fairyland. The motion picture empire grew up around him. Mrs. Baum remained at Ozcot, on Cherokee Avenue near Sunset Boulevard, until her death in 1953 at the age of 91. The house has since been torn down to make room for a modern apartment building.

As one would have expected, Baum was early fascinated by the artistic potential of the cinema. In 1908, while still living in Chicago, he had invested heavily in the production of a series of short, hand-colored movies depicting stories from his books. He called them "Radio Plays." They were presented in Chicago and later in New York with Baum standing by the screen to narrate the tales. He lost so heavily in this venture that in 1911 he found it necessary to file a bankruptcy petition in California, listing his debts as $12,600 and his assets as two suits of clothes and a typewriter.[17]

In 1913 Baum made another attempt to repeat the stage success of *The Wizard*. His musical *The Tik-Tok Man of Oz* opened in Los Angeles in 1913, then went on tour after profitable runs in

San Francisco and Chicago. The comedy team of James Morton and Frank Moore took the roles of Tik-Tok and Shaggy Man respectively. Queen Ann Soforth was played by Charlotte Greenwood. The play opened, like *The Wizard,* with the impressive sound and lighting effects of a violent storm; in this case the storm at sea that washes Betsy Bobbin of Oklahoma and Hank the mule to the shores of the Rose Kingdom. The book was written after the play, and dedicated to Louis F. Gottschalk who provided the play's musical score.

Although this was Baum's last stage success, his enthusiasm for the theater never left him. In later years he wrote and acted in musicals produced by the Uplifters, a Los Angeles social club that he helped found. The names of the officers were invented by him: Grand Muscle (president), Elevator (vice president), Royal Hoister (secretary), Lord High Raiser (treasurer), and the Excelsiors (directors). Will Rogers, George Arliss, and many other Hollywood notables later became members. Let us hope that some day someone will uplift the manuscript of *The Uplift of Lucifer,* one of the plays Baum wrote for this club.

In 1914 Baum turned his attention once more to motion pictures, forming the Oz Film Manufacturing Company to produce screen versions of his tales. In a press interview he explained that because of their many color plates his books had to sell at a price which kept them from millions of youngsters. Through the movies he hoped to make his stories available to every American boy and girl for the cost of admission to the theater—five cents. Like so many smaller film companies that were trying to get started at the time, Baum's company was soon backed against the wall by the competition of larger studios. Only five films were completed: *The Patchwork Girl of Oz* (played by Pierre Coudere, a French acrobat), *His Majesty the Scarecrow of Oz* (later retitled *The New Wizard of Oz*), *The Magic Cloak, The Last Egyptian,* and *The Gray Nun of Belgium.*

*The Wizard of Oz* was filmed as a one-reeler by Selig Pictures in 1910. Another silent version was issued in 1925 by Chadwick Pictures, starring the comedian Larry Semon as the Scarecrow. Oliver Hardy took the role of the tin man. And of course everyone has seen M-G-M's lavish technicolor spectacle, first released in 1939, with Judy Garland in the role of a singing Dorothy. Ray Bolger played the capering straw man, Jack Haley the Tin Woodman, and Bert Lahr an outrageously funny Cowardly Lion. Other roles included Billie Burke, badly miscast as Glinda, Frank Morgan as the Wizard, and the Singer Midgets as the Munchkins. The picture featured some excellent tunes (*Over the Rainbow* and *We're Off to See the Wizard*) and had several inspired touches, such as running the farm scenes in black and white to contrast them with the brilliant colors of Oz. But to my tastes the picture was marred by sentimentality toward the close and the inexcusable final revelation that the whole thing was a dream.

Baum's generous heart, unlike the fine velvet heart of the Tin Woodman, was not replaceable. Angina attacks and a gall bladder operation kept him in bed during the last year and a half of his life. *The Tin Woodman of Oz, The Magic of Oz,* and a rough draft of *Glinda of Oz* were written during this period. The latter book is almost devoid of humor. I have often fancied that the sunken island on which Dorothy was trapped beneath a lake was an unconscious expression of Baum's own sinking emotions. The island was raised when Dorothy thought of the proper magic words. There were no magic words for Baum's failing heart, and on May 6, 1919, at his home in Hollywood, it finally gave way. He was buried in Forest Lawn Memorial Park, at Glendale, where a simple monument bearing his name and dates of birth and death marks the resting place.

*Glinda of Oz,* edited by one of Baum's sons, was published posthumously. The next book in the series, *The Royal Book of Oz,* carries Baum's name on the cover and a statement inside by Mrs. Baum that her husband had left some unfinished notes for another Oz book. These notes, she says, were turned over to Ruth Plumly Thompson, then a twenty-year old Philadelphia journalist and children's author who had loved the Oz books as a child. All this seems to have been merely a device on the part of the publisher for easing the transition to a new author. The book was written entirely by Miss Thompson. She has since published eighteen additional Oz books, writing them with a zest and humor that has won her an ardent following.

# The Royal Historian of Oz

John Rea Neill, who illustrated all of Baum's Oz books except the first one, also tried his hand at three Oz books. He was not a skillful writer, but as the Royal Painter of Oz his pictures are as indissolubly linked with the Oz books as Tenniel's drawings are linked with Alice. Whatever one may think of Neill's pictures as works of art, there is no denying that he caught the full flavor of Baum's text, and his illustrations have exactly the sort of color and realism that Oz books require. Denslow's drawings for *The Wizard* possess a quaint wooden charm, but I have yet to meet an Oz enthusiast who regrets that Denslow did not carry on with the series.

Much can be said in praise of Miss Thompson's books and also of the most recent Oz book, written by Rachel Cosgrove; but in the opinion of many Oz fans the mantle of Royal Historian best fitted the shoulders of the late Jack Snow. His two Oz books are remarkable in capturing the mood and style of Baum. I have already mentioned his *Who's Who in Oz*, which contains lively biographies of every Oz character who ever appeared in an Oz book as well as biographical sketches of each Oz author and illustrator, and plot summaries of all the Oz books.[18]

Ray Bradbury has spoken many times of the influence of Oz on his career as a popular author of fantasy and science fiction. His story "The Exiles" pictures a future in which the psychologists have succeeded at last in destroying all books of fantasy. The narrative closes with the collapse of the Emerald City as the last Oz book goes up in flames.

But I do not think the Emerald City will collapse for a long, long time. A child's love of fantasy is too healthy a love. "Perhaps some of those big, grown-up people will poke fun at us," Baum wrote in his introduction to *A New Wonderland*, "—at you for reading these nonsense tales. . . . and at me for writing them. Never mind. Many of the big folk are still children—even as you and I. We can not measure a child by a standard of size or age. The big folk who are children will be our comrades; the others we need not consider at all, for they are self-exiled from our domain."

# Notes

1. From the *New York Mirror* (theatrical paper), June 24, 1882.
2. This story is told in a letter to me from Ralph Fletcher Seymour, a Chicago artist who knew Baum during his Chicago days.
3. One of Baum's most moving inscriptions is to be found in a presentation copy of this book to his sister, Mary Louise Baum Brewster:

   "My dear Mary: When I was young I longed to write a great novel that should win me fame. Now that I am getting old my first book is written to amuse children. For, aside from my evident inability to do anything 'great,' I have learned to regard fame as a will-o-the-wisp which, when caught, is not worth the possession; but to please a child is a sweet and lovely thing that warms one's heart and brings its own reward. I hope my book will succeed in that way—that the children will like it. You and I have inherited much the same temperament and literary taste and I know you will not despise these simple tales, but will understand me and accord me your full sympathy. Lovingly your brother Frank."
4. "We are revolting!" exclaims the leader of the Revolution to the Guardian of the Gates. To which he understandably replies, "You don't look it."
5. Mr. Seymour tells the story of this book's preparation in his privately printed autobiography, *Some Went this Way*, Chicago, 1945, p. 46.
6. A lengthy interview with Baum at his "Sign of the Goose"

appeared in the *Grand Rapids Herald,* August 18, 1907. There is a picture of Baum sitting in his goose chair, as well as photographs of the interior of the cottage.

7. A lengthy letter to Jack Snow in 1943, replying to 75 questions about her husband that Mr. Snow had asked in a previous letter.

8. This was not Baum's first attempt to collaborate with Tietjens and Denslow on a musical comedy. In 1901, at Tietjens' urging, he wrote the book of a comic opera titled *The Octopus* or *The Title Trust.* In Tietjens' unpublished diary, now in possession of his daughter, he describes their unsuccessful attempts to find a producer. Baum was particularly fond of the song "I am a Great Promoter," to be sung by Gripem Harde. There are references to other songs, but unfortunately no intimations of plot. The diary also contains many details about the wrangling of the three men over the contract for their second effort, *The Wizard,* and speaks of "much friction" between Baum and the producer, Julian Mitchell. Nothing came of later comic opera projects— *Father Goose, Prince Silver Wings,* and *The Pagan Potentate* —on which Tietjens and Baum planned to work jointly.

9. From *In Other Lands than Ours,* a collection of Mrs. Baum's letters from abroad, privately printed by her husband in 1907.

10. *Cf.* the following paragraph of a letter dated June 7, 1943, from Baum's nephew, Henry B. Brewster, of Syracuse, N.Y., to Jack Snow: "Mr. Baum always liked to tell wild tales, with a perfectly straight face, and earnestly, as though he really believed them himself. . . . His mother was very religious . . . and felt she knew her Bible very well. Frank Baum seemed to take particular delight in teasing her and I recall, not once but many times, how he would pretend to quote from the Bible, with which he definitely was not familiar. For example, once she said, 'Frank, you are telling a story,' and he said, 'Well, Mother, as you know, in St. Paul's epistle to the Ephesians he said, "All men are liars." ' Whereupon his mother said, 'Why, Frank, you are wrong, I do not recall

that,' and irrespective of the fact that she had been fooled so many times she would look up her Bible to see if she were wrong, and he right. Frank Baum was one of the most imaginative of men. There was nothing wrong, but he did love to 'Fairytale,' or as you might say, tell 'white lies.' "

11. From her letter to Jack Snow, *op. cit.*

12. *Ibid.*

13. *Ibid.*

14. "It is possible for beasts—or even people—to be destroyed, but the task is so difficult that it is seldom attempted. Because it is free from sickness and death is one reason why Oz is a fairyland, but it is doubtful whether those who come to Oz from the outside world. . . . will live forever or cannot be injured. Even Ozma is not sure about this, and so the guests of Ozma from other lands are always carefully protected from any danger, so as to be on the safe side."—*The Magic of Oz,* p. 83.

15. The ultimate ideal of Marxian socialism, after the state has withered away, is of course an anarchist society. This explains an article in *New Masses,* Oct. 4, 1938, titled "The Red Wizard of Oz." Stewart Robb, the author, had just discovered that Oz books had been banned from all New York City libraries and he satirically suggests that the reason may be a political one. Another letter of Robb's, in the *New York Post,* Oct. 9, 1938, compares the late Frank ("I am the law") Hague, then mayor and political boss of Jersey City, to The Supreme Dictator of the Flatheads (*Glinda of Oz*). The Supreme Dictator keeps getting reelected because of a law that gives himself the authority to count the votes. Both letters appear in Robb's privately published book *Letters on Nostradamus,* New York, no date.

16. "The Wizard of Chittenango," by James Thurber, *The New Republic,* Dec. 12, 1934.

17. *Chicago Tribune,* Aug. 16, 1911.

18. With one exception, *The Laughing Dragon of Oz,* by Baum's son, Frank Joslyn. This was issued by Whitman Publishing Company in 1934, as one of their "Big Little Book Series,"

and sold in the dime stores for ten cents. His second book, *The Enchanted Princess of Oz,* was purchased by Whitman but never published. No characters from previous Oz books appear in either work.

Mention also should be made of two "Oz" books published by Denslow. He and Baum parted company over a disagreement as to how much the illustrations had contributed to the success of the first Oz book and its musical. Feeling that he was in part a creator of Oz, and legally in possession of a copyright on his illustrations, Denslow wrote and illustrated a picture book titled *Scarecrow and the Tin Man* (New York: G. W. Dillingham, 1904) telling how the two men escape from a New York theater in which they are appearing, and of the mishaps that befall them before the police send them back to the theater. Denslow also issued a 43-page booklet of color plates from the first Oz book. It was called *Pictures from the Wonderful Wizard of Oz* (Chicago: George W. Ogilvie, no date) and carried his own name on the title page but no mention of Baum. Accompanying the pictures is a story by Thomas H. Russell about the adventures of a "Little Girl" with the Scarecrow and the Tin Man. Neither of these books contains the word "Oz."

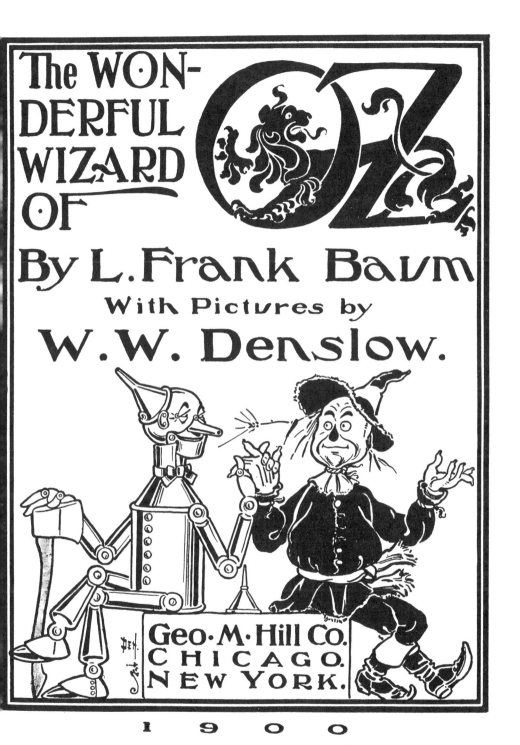

The WON-
DERFUL
WIZARD
OF Oz

By L. Frank Baum

With Pictures by

W. W. Denslow.

Geo. M. Hill Co.
CHICAGO.
NEW YORK.

1 9 0 0

[TITLE PAGE OF ORIGINAL EDITION]

# List of Chapters

## List of Chapters

*This book is dedicated to my
good friend & comrade
My Wife*

L. F. B.

## Introduction

FOLK lore, legends, myths and fairy tales have followed child-hood through the ages, for every healthy youngster has a whole-some and instinctive love for stories fantastic, marvelous and manifestly unreal. The winged fairies of Grimm and Andersen have brought more happiness to childish hearts than all other human creations.

Yet the old-time fairy tale, having served for generations, may now be classed as "historical" in the children's library; for the time has come for a series of newer "wonder tales" in which the stereo-typed genie, dwarf and fairy are eliminated, together with all the horrible and bloodcurdling incident devised by their authors to point a fearsome moral to each tale. Modern education includes morality; therefore the modern child seeks only entertainment in its wonder-tales and gladly dispenses with all disagreeable incident.

Having this thought in mind, the story of "The Wonderful Wizard of Oz" was written solely to pleasure children of today. It aspires to being a modernized fairy tale, in which the wonderment and joy are retained and the heart-aches and nightmares are left out.

L. FRANK BAUM

Chicago, April, 1900

*"She caught Toto by the ear."*

# *The Cyclone*

DOROTHY lived in the midst of the great Kansas prairies, with Uncle Henry, who was a farmer, and Aunt Em, who was the farmer's wife. Their house was small, for the lumber to build it had to be carried by wagon many miles. There were four walls, a floor and a roof, which made one room; and this room contained a rusty looking cooking stove, a cupboard for the dishes, a table, three or four chairs, and the beds. Uncle Henry and Aunt Em had a big bed in one corner, and Dorothy a little bed in another corner. There was no garret at all, and no cellar—except a small hole, dug in the ground, called a cyclone cellar, where the family could go in case one of those great whirlwinds arose, mighty enough to crush any building in its path. It was reached by a trap-door in the middle of the floor, from which a ladder led down into the small, dark hole.

When Dorothy stood in the doorway and looked around, she could see nothing but the great gray[1] prairie on every side. Not a tree nor a house broke the broad sweep of flat country that reached the edge of the sky in all directions. The sun had baked the plowed land into a gray mass, with little cracks running through it. Even the grass was not green, for the sun had burned the tops of the long blades until they were the same gray color to be seen everywhere. Once the house had been painted, but the sun blistered the paint and the rains washed it away, and now the house was as dull and gray as everything else.

When Aunt Em came there to live she was a young, pretty wife. The sun and wind had changed her, too. They had taken the sparkle from her eyes and left them a sober gray; they had taken the red from her cheeks and lips, and they were gray also. She was thin and gaunt, and never smiled, now. When Dorothy, who was an orphan, first came to her, Aunt Em had been so startled by the child's laughter that she would scream and press her hand upon her heart whenever Dorothy's merry voice reached her ears; and she still looked at the little girl with wonder that she could find anything to laugh at.

Uncle Henry never laughed. He worked hard from morning till night and did not know what joy was. He was gray also, from his long beard to his rough boots, and he looked stern and solemn, and rarely spoke.

It was Toto that made Dorothy laugh, and saved her from growing as gray as her other surroundings. Toto was not gray; he was a little black dog, with long, silky hair and small black eyes that twinkled merrily on either side of his funny, wee nose. Toto played all day long, and Dorothy played with him, and loved him dearly.

To-day, however, they were not playing. Uncle Henry sat upon the door-step and looked anxiously at the sky, which was even grayer than usual. Dorothy stood in the door with Toto in her arms, and looked at the sky too. Aunt Em was washing the dishes.

From the far north they heard a low wail of the wind, and Uncle Henry and Dorothy could see where the long grass bowed in waves before the coming storm. There now came a sharp whistling in the air from the south, and as they turned their eyes that way they saw ripples in the grass coming from that direction also.

Suddenly Uncle Henry stood up.

"There's a cyclone coming, Em," he called to his wife; "I'll go look after the stock." Then he ran toward the sheds where the cows and horses were kept.

Aunt Em dropped her work and came to the door. One glance told her of the danger close at hand.

"Quick, Dorothy!" she screamed; "run for the cellar!"

Toto jumped out of Dorothy's arms and hid under the bed, and the girl started to get him. Aunt Em, badly frightened, threw open the trap-door in the floor and climbed down the ladder into the small, dark hole. Dorothy caught Toto at last, and started to follow her aunt. When she was half way across the room there came a great shriek from the wind, and the house shook so hard that she lost her footing and sat down suddenly upon the floor.

A strange thing then happened.

# The Cyclone

The house whirled around two or three times and rose slowly through the air. Dorothy felt as if she were going up in a balloon.

The north and south winds met where the house stood, and made it the exact center of the cyclone. In the middle of a cyclone the air is generally still, but the great pressure of the wind on every side of the house raised it up higher and higher, until it was at the very top of the cyclone; and there it remained and was carried miles and miles away as easily as you could carry a feather.

It was very dark, and the wind howled horribly around her, but Dorothy found she was riding quite easily. After the first few whirls around, and one other time when the house tipped badly, she felt as if she were being rocked gently, like a baby in a cradle.

Toto did not like it. He ran about the room, now here, now there, barking loudly; but Dorothy sat quite still on the floor and waited to see what would happen.

Once Toto got too near the open trap-door, and fell in; and at first the little girl thought she had lost him. But soon she saw one of his ears sticking up through the hole, for the strong pressure of the air was keeping him up so that he could not fall. She crept to the hole, caught Toto by the ear, and dragged him into the room again; afterward closing the trap-door so that no more accidents could happen.

Hour after hour passed away, and slowly Dorothy got over her fright; but she felt quite lonely, and the wind shrieked so loudly all about her that she nearly became deaf. At first she had wondered if she would be dashed to pieces when the house fell again; but as the hours passed and nothing terrible happened, she stopped worrying and resolved to wait calmly and see what the future would bring. At last she crawled over the swaying floor to her bed, and lay down upon it; and Toto followed and lay down beside her.

In spite of the swaying of the house and the wailing of the wind, Dorothy soon closed her eyes and fell fast asleep.

# The Council with the Munchkins

SHE was awakened by a shock, so sudden and severe that if Dorothy had not been lying on the soft bed she might have been hurt. As it was, the jar made her catch her breath and wonder what had happened; and Toto put his cold little nose into her face and whined dismally. Dorothy sat up and noticed that the house was not moving; nor was it dark, for the bright sunshine came in at the window, flooding the little room. She sprang from her bed and with Toto at her heels ran and opened the door.

The little girl gave a cry of amazement and looked about her, her eyes growing bigger and bigger at the wonderful sights she saw.

The cyclone had set the house down, very gently—for a cyclone —in the midst of a country of marvelous beauty. There were lovely patches of green sward all about, with stately trees bearing rich and luscious fruits. Banks of gorgeous flowers were on every hand, and birds with rare and brilliant plumage sang and fluttered in the trees and bushes. A little way off was a small brook, rushing and sparkling along between green banks, and murmuring in a voice very grateful to a little girl who had lived so long on the dry, gray prairies.

While she stood looking eagerly at the strange and beautiful sights, she noticed coming toward her a group of the queerest people she had ever seen. They were not as big as the grown folk she had always been used to; but neither were they very small. In fact, they seemed about as tall as Dorothy, who was a well-grown child for her age, although they were, so far as looks go, many years older.

Three were men and one a woman, and all were oddly dressed. They wore round hats that rose to a small point a foot above their heads, with little bells around the brims that tinkled sweetly as they moved. The hats of the men were blue; the little woman's hat was white, and she wore a white gown that hung in plaits from her shoulders; over it were sprinkled little stars that glistened in the sun like diamonds. The men were dressed in blue, of the same shade as their hats, and wore well polished boots with a deep roll of blue at the tops. The men, Dorothy thought, were about as old as Uncle Henry, for two of them had beards. But the little woman was doubtless much older: her face was covered with wrinkles, her hair was nearly white, and she walked rather stiffly.

When these people drew near the house where Dorothy was standing in the doorway, they paused and whispered among themselves, as if afraid to come farther. But the little old woman walked up to Dorothy, made a low bow and said, in a sweet voice,

"You are welcome, most noble Sorceress, to the land of the Munchkins. We are so grateful to you for having killed the Wicked Witch of the East, and for setting our people free from bondage."

Dorothy listened to this speech with wonder. What could the little woman possibly mean by calling her a sorceress, and saying she had killed the Wicked Witch of the East? Dorothy was an innocent, harmless little girl, who had been carried by a cyclone many miles from home; and she had never killed anything in all her life.

But the little woman evidently expected her to answer; so Dorothy said, with hesitation,

"You are very kind; but there must be some mistake. I have not killed anything."

"Your house did, anyway," replied the little old woman with a laugh; "and that is the same thing. See!" she continued, pointing to the corner of the house; "there are her two toes, still sticking out from under a block of wood."

Dorothy looked, and gave a little cry of fright. There, indeed, just under the corner of the great beam the house rested on, two feet were sticking out, shod in silver shoes with pointed toes.

"Oh, dear! oh, dear!" cried Dorothy, clasping her hands together in dismay; "the house must have fallen on her. What ever shall we do?"

"There is nothing to be done," said the little woman, calmly.

"But who was she?" asked Dorothy.

"She was the Wicked Witch of the East, as I said," answered the little woman. "She has held all the Munchkins in bondage for many years, making them slave for her night and day. Now they are all set free, and are grateful to you for the favour."

"Who are the Munchkins?" enquired Dorothy.

"They are the people who live in this land of the East,[2] where the Wicked Witch ruled."

"Are you a Munchkin?" asked Dorothy.

"No; but I am their friend, although I live in the land of the North.[3] When they saw the Witch of the East was dead the Munchkins sent a swift messenger to me, and I came at once. I am the Witch of the North."

"Oh, gracious!" cried Dorothy; "are you a real witch?"

"Yes, indeed," answered the little woman. "But I am a good witch, and the people love me. I am not as powerful as the Wicked Witch was who ruled here, or I should have set the people free myself."

"But I thought all witches were wicked," said the girl, who was half frightened at facing a real witch.

"Oh, no; that is a great mistake. There were only four witches in all the Land of Oz, and two of them, those who live in the North and the South, are good witches. I know this is true, for I am one of them myself, and cannot be mistaken. Those who dwelt in the East and the West were, indeed, wicked witches; but now that you have killed one of them, there is but one Wicked Witch in all the Land of Oz—the one who lives in the West."

"But," said Dorothy, after a moment's thought, "Aunt Em has told me that the witches were all dead—years and years ago."

"Who is Aunt Em?" enquired the little old woman.

"She is my aunt who lives in Kansas, where I came from."

The Witch of the North seemed to think for a time, with her head bowed and her eyes upon the ground. Then she looked up and said,

"I do not know where Kansas is, for I have never heard that country mentioned before. But tell me, is it a civilized country?"

"Oh, yes," replied Dorothy.

"Then that accounts for it. In the civilized countries I believe there are no witches left; nor wizards, nor sorceresses, nor magicians. But, you see, the Land of Oz has never been civilized, for we are cut off from all the rest of the world. Therefore we still have witches and wizards amongst us."

"Who are the Wizards?" asked Dorothy.

"Oz himself is the Great Wizard," answered the Witch, sinking her voice to a whisper. "He is more powerful than all the rest of us together. He lives in the City of Emeralds."

Dorothy was going to ask another question, but just then the Munchkins, who had been standing silently by, gave a loud shout and pointed to the corner of the house where the Wicked Witch had been lying.

"What is it?" asked the little old woman; and looked, and began to laugh. The feet of the dead Witch had disappeared entirely and nothing was left but the silver shoes.

"She was so old," exclaimed the Witch of the North, "that she dried up quickly in the sun. That is the end of her. But the silver shoes are yours, and you shall have them to wear." She reached down and picked up the shoes, and after shaking the dust out of them handed them to Dorothy.

"The Witch of the East was proud of those silver shoes," said one of the Munchkins; "and there is some charm connected with them; but what it is we never knew."

Dorothy carried the shoes into the house and placed them on the table. Then she came out again to the Munchkins and said,

"I am anxious to get back to my Aunt and Uncle, for I am sure they will worry about me. Can you help me find my way?"

The Munchkins and the Witch first looked at one another, and then at Dorothy, and then shook their heads.

"At the East, not far from here," said one, "there is a great desert, and none could live to cross it."

"It is the same at the South," said another, "for I have been there and seen it. The South is the country of the Quadlings."

# The Council with the Munchkins

"I am told," said the third man, "that it is the same at the West. And that country, where the Winkies live, is ruled by the Wicked Witch of the West, who would make you her slave if you passed her way."

"The North is my home," said the old lady, "and at its edge is the same great desert that surrounds this Land of Oz. I'm afraid, my dear, you will have to live with us."

Dorothy began to sob, at this, for she felt lonely among all these strange people. Her tears seemed to grieve the kind-hearted Munchkins, for they immediately took out their handkerchiefs and began to weep also. As for the little old woman, she took off her cap and balanced the point on the end of her nose, while she counted "one, two, three" in a solemn voice. At once the cap changed to a slate, on which was written in big, white chalk marks:

"LET DOROTHY GO TO THE CITY OF EMERALDS."

The little old woman took the slate from her nose, and having read the words on it, asked,

"Is your name Dorothy, my dear?"

"Yes," answered the child, looking up and drying her tears.

"Then you must go to the City of Emeralds. Perhaps Oz will help you."

"Where is this City?" asked Dorothy.

"It is exactly in the center of the country, and is ruled by Oz, the Great Wizard I told you of."

"Is he a good man?" enquired the girl, anxiously.

"He is a good Wizard. Whether he is a man or not I cannot tell, for I have never seen him."

"How can I get there?" asked Dorothy.

"You must walk. It is a long journey, through a country that is sometimes pleasant and sometimes dark and terrible. However, I will use all the magic arts I know of to keep you from harm."

"Won't you go with me?" pleaded the girl, who had begun to look upon the little old woman as her only friend.

"No, I cannot do that," she replied; "but I will give you my kiss, and no one will dare injure a person who has been kissed by the Witch of the North."

She came close to Dorothy and kissed her gently on the forehead.

Where her lips touched the girl they left a round, shining mark, as Dorothy found out soon after.

"The road to the City of Emeralds is paved with yellow brick,"[4] said the Witch; "so you cannot miss it. When you get to Oz do not be afraid of him, but tell your story and ask him to help you. Good-bye, my dear."

The three Munchkins bowed low to her and wished her a pleasant journey, after which they walked away through the trees. The Witch gave Dorothy a friendly little nod, whirled around on her left heel three times, and straightway disappeared, much to the surprise of little Toto, who barked after her loudly enough when she had gone, because he had been afraid even to growl while she stood by.

But Dorothy, knowing her to be a witch, had expected her to disappear in just that way, and was not surprised in the least.

*"Dorothy gazed thoughtfully at the Scarecrow."*

# How Dorothy Saved
# the Scarecrow

W HEN Dorothy was left alone she began to feel hungry. So she went to the cupboard and cut herself some bread, which she spread with butter. She gave some to Toto, and taking a pail from the shelf she carried it down to the little brook and filled it with clear, sparkling water. Toto ran over to the trees and began to bark at the birds sitting there. Dorothy went to get him, and saw such delicious fruit hanging from the branches that she gathered some of it, finding it just what she wanted to help out her breakfast.

Then she went back to the house, and having helped herself and Toto to a good drink of the cool, clear water, she set about making ready for the journey to the City of Emeralds.

Dorothy had only one other dress, but that happened to be clean and was hanging on a peg beside her bed. It was gingham, with checks of white and blue; and although the blue was somewhat faded with many washings, it was still a pretty frock. The girl washed herself carefully, dressed herself in the clean gingham, and tied her pink sunbonnet on her head. She took a little basket and filled it with bread from the cupboard, laying a white cloth over the top. Then she looked down at her feet and noticed how old and worn her shoes were.

"They surely will never do for a long journey, Toto," she said. And Toto looked up into her face with his little black eyes and wagged his tail to show he knew what she meant.

At that moment Dorothy saw lying on the table the silver shoes that had belonged to the Witch of the East.

"I wonder if they will fit me," she said to Toto. "They would be just the thing to take a long walk in, for they could not wear out."

She took off her old leather shoes and tried on the silver ones, which fitted her as well as if they had been made for her.

Finally she picked up her basket.

"Come along, Toto," she said, "we will go to the Emerald City and ask the great Oz how to get back to Kansas again."

She closed the door, locked it, and put the key carefully in the pocket of her dress.[5] And so, with Toto trotting along soberly behind her, she started on her journey.

There were several roads near by, but it did not take her long to find the one paved with yellow brick. Within a short time she was walking briskly toward the Emerald City, her silver shoes tinkling merrily on the hard, yellow roadbed. The sun shone bright and the birds sang sweet and Dorothy did not feel nearly as bad as you might think a little girl would who had been suddenly whisked away from her own country and set down in the midst of a strange land.

She was surprised, as she walked along, to see how pretty the country was about her. There were neat fences at the sides of the road, painted a dainty blue color, and beyond them were fields of grain and vegetables in abundance. Evidently the Munchkins were good farmers and able to raise large crops. Once in a while she would pass a house, and the people came out to look at her and bow low as she went by; for everyone knew she had been the means of destroying the Wicked Witch and setting them free from bondage. The houses of the Munchkins were odd looking dwellings, for each was round, with a big dome for a roof. All were painted blue, for in this country of the East blue was the favorite color.

Toward evening, when Dorothy was tired with her long walk and began to wonder where she should pass the night, she came to a house rather larger than the rest. On the green lawn before it many men and women were dancing. Five little fiddlers played as loudly as possible and the people were laughing and singing, while a big table near by was loaded with delicious fruits and nuts, pies and cakes, and many other good things to eat.

The people greeted Dorothy kindly, and invited her to supper and to pass the night with them; for this was the home of one of the richest Munchkins in the land, and his friends were gathered with him to celebrate their freedom from the bondage of the Wicked Witch.

Dorothy ate a hearty supper and was waited upon by the rich Munchkin himself, whose name was Boq. Then she sat down upon a settee and watched the people dance.

When Boq saw her silver shoes he said,

"You must be a great sorceress."

"Why?" asked the girl.

"Because you wear silver shoes and have killed the Wicked Witch. Besides you have white in your frock, and only witches and sorceresses wear white."

"My dress is blue and white checked," said Dorothy, smoothing out the wrinkles in it.

"It is kind of you to wear that," said Boq. "Blue is the color of the Munchkins, and white is the witch color; so we know you are a friendly witch."

Dorothy did not know what to say to this, for all the people seemed to think her a witch, and she knew very well she was only an ordinary little girl who had come by the chance of a cyclone into a strange land.

When she had tired watching the dancing, Boq led her into the house, where he gave her a room with a pretty bed in it. The sheets were made of blue cloth, and Dorothy slept soundly in them till morning, with Toto curled up on the blue rug beside her.

She ate a hearty breakfast, and watched a wee Munchkin baby, who played with Toto and pulled his tail and crowed and laughed in a way that greatly amused Dorothy. Toto was a fine curiosity to all the people, for they had never seen a dog before.

"How far is it to the Emerald City?" the girl asked.

"I do not know," answered Boq, gravely, "for I have never been there. It is better for people to keep away from Oz, unless they have business with him. But it is a long way to the Emerald City, and it will take you many days. The country here is rich and pleasant, but you must pass through rough and dangerous places before you reach the end of your journey."

This worried Dorothy a little, but she knew that only the great Oz could help her get to Kansas again, so she bravely resolved not to turn back.

She bade her friends good-bye, and again started along the road of yellow brick. When she had gone several miles she thought she would stop to rest, and so climbed to the top of the fence beside the road and sat down. There was a great cornfield beyond the fence, and not far away she saw a Scarecrow, placed high on a pole to keep the birds from the ripe corn.

Dorothy leaned her chin upon her hand and gazed thoughtfully at the Scarecrow. Its head was a small sack stuffed with straw, with eyes, nose and mouth painted on it to represent a face. An old, pointed blue hat, that had belonged to some Munchkin, was perched on this head, and the rest of the figure was a blue suit of clothes, worn and faded, which had also been stuffed with straw. On the feet were some old boots with blue tops, such as every man wore in this country, and the figure was raised above the stalks of corn by means of the pole stuck up its back.

While Dorothy was looking earnestly into the queer, painted face of the Scarecrow, she was surprised to see one of the eyes slowly wink at her. She thought she must have been mistaken, at first, for none of the scarecrows in Kansas ever wink; but presently the figure nodded its head to her in a friendly way. Then she climbed down from the fence and walked up to it, while Toto ran around the pole and barked.

"Good day," said the Scarecrow, in a rather husky voice.

"Did you speak?" asked the girl, in wonder.

"Certainly," answered the Scarecrow; "how do you do?"

"I'm pretty well, thank you," replied Dorothy, politely; "how do you do?"

"I'm not feeling well," said the Scarecrow, with a smile, "for it is very tedious being perched up here night and day to scare away crows."

"Can't you get down?" asked Dorothy.

# How Dorothy Saved the Scarecrow

"No, for this pole is stuck up my back. If you will please take away the pole I shall be greatly obliged to you."

Dorothy reached up both arms and lifted the figure off the pole; for, being stuffed with straw, it was quite light.

"Thank you very much," said the Scarecrow, when he had been set down on the ground. "I feel like a new man."

Dorothy was puzzled at this, for it sounded queer to hear a stuffed man speak, and to see him bow and walk along beside her.

"Who are you?" asked the Scarecrow, when he had stretched himself and yawned, "and where are you going?"

"My name is Dorothy," said the girl, "and I am going to the Emerald City, to ask the great Oz to send me back to Kansas."

"Where is the Emerald City?" he enquired; "and who is Oz?"

"Why don't you know?" she returned, in surprise.

"No, indeed; I don't know anything. You see, I am stuffed, so I have no brains at all," he answered, sadly.

"Oh," said Dorothy; "I'm awfully sorry for you."

"Do you think," he asked, "if I go to the Emerald City with you, that the great Oz would give me some brains?"

"I cannot tell," she returned; "but you may come with me, if you like. If Oz will not give you any brains you will be no worse off than you are now."

"That is true," said the Scarecrow. "You see," he continued, confidentially, "I don't mind my legs and arms and body being stuffed, because I cannot get hurt. If anyone treads on my toes or sticks a pin into me, it doesn't matter for I can't feel it. But I do not want people to call me a fool, and if my head stays stuffed with straw instead of with brains, as yours is, how am I ever to know anything?"

"I understand how you feel," said the little girl, who was truly sorry for him. "If you will come with me I'll ask Oz to do all he can for you."

"Thank you," he answered, gratefully.

They walked back to the road, Dorothy helped him over the fence, and they started along the path of yellow brick for the Emerald City.

Toto did not like this addition to the party, at first. He smelled around the stuffed man as if he suspected there might be a nest of rats in the straw, and he often growled in an unfriendly way at the Scarecrow.

"Don't mind Toto," said Dorothy, to her new friend; "he never bites."

"Oh, I'm not afraid," replied the Scarecrow, "he can't hurt the straw. Do let me carry that basket for you. I shall not mind it, for I can't get tired. I'll tell you a secret," he continued, as he walked along; "there is only one thing in the world I am afraid of."

"What is that?" asked Dorothy; "the Munchkin farmer who made you?"

"No," answered the Scarecrow; "it's a lighted match."

# The Road Through the Forest

AFTER a few hours the road began to be rough, and the walking grew so difficult that the Scarecrow often stumbled over the yellow brick, which were here very uneven. Sometimes, indeed, they were broken or missing altogether, leaving holes that Toto jumped across and Dorothy walked around. As for the Scarecrow, having no brains he walked straight ahead, and so stepped into the holes and fell at full length on the hard bricks. It never hurt him, however, and Dorothy would pick him up and set him upon his feet again, while he joined her in laughing merrily at his own mishap.

The farms were not nearly so well cared for here as they were farther back. There were fewer houses and fewer fruit trees, and the farther they went the more dismal and lonesome the country became.

At noon they sat down by the roadside, near a little brook, and Dorothy opened her basket and got out some bread. She offered a piece to the Scarecrow, but he refused.

"I am never hungry," he said; "and it is a lucky thing I am not. For my mouth is only painted, and if I should cut a hole in it so I could eat, the straw I am stuffed with would come out, and that would spoil the shape of my head."

Dorothy saw at once that this was true, so she only nodded and went on eating her bread.

"Tell me something about yourself, and the country you came from," said the Scarecrow, when she had finished her dinner. So she told him all about Kansas, and how gray everything was there, and how the cyclone had carried her to this queer Land of Oz. The Scarecrow listened carefully, and said,

"I cannot understand why you should wish to leave this beautiful country and go back to the dry, gray place you call Kansas."

"That is because you have no brains," answered the girl. "No matter how dreary and gray our homes are, we people of flesh and blood would rather live there than in any other country, be it ever so beautiful. There is no place like home."

The Scarecrow sighed.

"Of course I cannot understand it," he said. "If your heads were stuffed with straw, like mine, you would probably all live in the beautiful places, and then Kansas would have no people at all. It is fortunate for Kansas that you have brains."

"Won't you tell me a story, while we are resting?" asked the child.

The Scarecrow looked at her reproachfully, and answered,

"My life has been so short that I really know nothing whatever. I was only made day before yesterday. What happened in the world before that time is all unknown to me. Luckily, when the farmer made my head, one of the first things he did was to paint my ears, so that I heard what was going on. There was another Munchkin with him, and the first thing I heard was the farmer saying,

" 'How do you like those ears?'

" 'They aren't straight,' answered the other.

" 'Never mind,' said the farmer; 'they are ears just the same,' which was true enough.

" 'Now I'll make the eyes,' said the farmer. So he painted my right eye, and as soon as it was finished I found myself looking at him and at everything around me with a great deal of curiosity, for this was my first glimpse of the world.

" 'That's a rather pretty eye,' remarked the Munchkin who was watching the farmer; 'blue paint is just the color for eyes.'

" 'I think I'll make the other a little bigger,'[6] said the farmer; and when the second eye was done I could see much better than before. Then he made my nose and my mouth; but I did not speak, because at that time I didn't know what a mouth was for. I had the fun of watching them make my body and my arms and legs; and when they fastened on my head, at last, I felt very proud, for I thought I was just as good a man as anyone.

" 'This fellow will scare the crows fast enough,' said the farmer; 'he looks just like a man.'

" 'Why he is a man,' said the other, and I quite agreed with him. The farmer carried me under his arm to the cornfield, and set me up on a tall stick, where you found me. He and his friend soon after walked away and left me alone.

"I did not like to be deserted this way; so I tried to walk after them, but my feet would not touch the ground, and I was forced to stay on that pole. It was a lonely life to lead, for I had nothing to think of, having been made such a little while before. Many crows and other birds flew into the cornfield, but as soon as they saw me they flew away again, thinking I was a Munchkin; and this pleased me and made me feel that I was quite an important person. By and by an old crow flew near me, and after looking at me carefully he perched upon my shoulder and said,

" 'I wonder if that farmer thought to fool me in this clumsy manner. Any crow of sense could see that you are only stuffed with straw.' Then he hopped down at my feet and ate all the corn he wanted. The other birds, seeing he was not harmed by me, came to eat the corn too, so in a short time there was a great flock of them about me.

"I felt sad at this, for it showed I was not such a good Scarecrow after all; but the old crow comforted me, saying: 'If you only had brains in your head you would be as good a man as any of them, and a better man than some of them. Brains are the only things worth having in this world, no matter whether one is a crow or a man.'

"After the crows had gone I thought this over, and decided I would try hard to get some brains. By good luck, you came along and pulled me off the stake, and from what you say I am sure the great Oz will give me brains as soon as we get to the Emerald City."

"I hope so," said Dorothy, earnestly, "since you seem anxious to have them."

"Oh, yes; I am anxious," returned the Scarecrow. "It is such an uncomfortable feeling to know one is a fool."

"Well," said the girl, "let us go." And she handed the basket to the Scarecrow.

There were no fences at all by the road side now, and the land was rough and untilled. Toward evening they came to a great forest, where the trees grew so big and close together that their branches met over the road of yellow brick. It was almost dark under the trees, for the branches shut out the daylight; but the travellers did not stop, and went on into the forest.

"If this road goes in, it must come out," said the Scarecrow, "and as the Emerald City is at the other end of the road, we must go wherever it leads us."

"Anyone would know that," said Dorothy.

"Certainly; that is why I know it," returned the Scarecrow. "If it required brains to figure it out, I never should have said it."

After an hour or so the light faded away, and they found themselves stumbling along in the darkness. Dorothy could not see at all, but Toto could, for some dogs see very well in the dark; and the Scarecrow declared he could see as well as by day. So she took hold of his arm, and managed to get along fairly well.

"If you see any house, or any place where we can pass the night," she said, "you must tell me; for it is very uncomfortable walking in the dark."

Soon after the Scarecrow stopped.

"I see a little cottage at the right of us," he said, "built of logs and branches. Shall we go there?"

"Yes, indeed," answered the child. "I am all tired out."

So the Scarecrow led her through the trees until they reached the cottage, and Dorothy entered and found a bed of dried leaves in one corner. She lay down at once, and with Toto beside her soon fell into a sound sleep. The Scarecrow, who was never tired, stood up in another corner and waited patiently until morning came.

*" 'This is a great comfort,' said the Tin Woodman."*

# The Rescue of the Tin Woodman

WHEN Dorothy awoke the sun was shining through the trees and Toto had long been out chasing birds and squirrels. She sat up and looked around her. There was the Scarecrow, still standing patiently in his corner, waiting for her.

"We must go and search for water," she said to him.

"Why do you want water?" he asked.

"To wash my face clean after the dust of the road, and to drink, so the dry bread will not stick in my throat."

"It must be inconvenient to be made of flesh," said the Scarecrow, thoughtfully; "for you must sleep, and eat and drink. However, you have brains, and it is worth a lot of bother to be able to think properly."

They left the cottage and walked through the trees until they found a little spring of clear water, where Dorothy drank and bathed and ate her breakfast. She saw there was not much bread left in the basket, and the girl was thankful the Scarecrow did not have to eat anything, for there was scarcely enough for herself and Toto for the day.

When she had finished her meal, and was about to go back to the road of yellow brick, she was startled to hear a deep groan near by.

"What was that?" she asked, timidly.

"I cannot imagine," replied the Scarecrow; "but we can go and see."

Just then another groan reached their ears, and the sound seemed to come from behind them. They turned and walked through the forest a few steps, when Dorothy discovered something shining in a ray of sunshine that fell between the trees. She ran to the place, and then stopped short, with a cry of surprise.

One of the big trees had been partly chopped through, and standing beside it, with an uplifted axe in his hands, was a man made entirely of tin. His head and arms and legs were jointed upon his body, but he stood perfectly motionless, as if he could not stir at all.

Dorothy looked at him in amazement, and so did the Scarecrow, while Toto barked sharply and made a snap at the tin legs, which hurt his teeth.

"Did you groan?" asked Dorothy.

"Yes," answered the tin man; "I did. I've been groaning for more than a year, and no one has ever heard me before or come to help me."

"What can I do for you?" she enquired, softly, for she was moved by the sad voice in which the man spoke.

"Get an oil-can and oil my joints," he answered. "They are rusted so badly that I cannot move them at all; if I am well oiled I shall soon be all right again. You will find an oil-can on a shelf in my cottage."

Dorothy at once ran back to the cottage and found the oil-can, and then she returned and asked, anxiously, "Where are your joints?"

"Oil my neck, first," replied the Tin Woodman. So she oiled it, and as it was quite badly rusted the Scarecrow took hold of the tin head and moved it gently from side to side until it worked freely, and then the man could turn it himself.

"Now oil the joints in my arms," he said. And Dorothy oiled them and the Scarecrow bent them carefully until they were quite free from rust and as good as new.

The Tin Woodman gave a sigh of satisfaction and lowered his axe, which he leaned against the tree.

"This is a great comfort," he said. "I have been holding that axe in the air ever since I rusted, and I'm glad to be able to put it down at last. Now, if you will oil the joints of my legs, I shall be all right once more."

So they oiled his legs until he could move them freely; and he thanked them again and again for his release, for he seemed a very polite creature, and very grateful.

"I might have stood there always if you had not come along," he said; "so you have certainly saved my life. How did you happen to be here?"

"We are on our way to the Emerald City, to see the great Oz," she answered, "and we stopped at your cottage to pass the night."

"Why do you wish to see Oz?" he asked.

"I want him to send me back to Kansas; and the Scarecrow wants him to put a few brains into his head," she replied.

The Tin Woodman appeared to think deeply for a moment. Then he said:

"Do you suppose Oz could give me a heart?"

"Why, I guess so," Dorothy answered; "it would be as easy as to give the Scarecrow brains."

"True," the Tin Woodman returned. "So, if you will allow me to join your party, I will also go to the Emerald City and ask Oz to help me."

"Come along," said the Scarecrow, heartily; and Dorothy added that she would be pleased to have his company. So the Tin Woodman shouldered his axe and they all passed through the forest until they came to the road that was paved with yellow brick.

The Tin Woodman had asked Dorothy to put the oil-can in her basket. "For," he said, "if I should get caught in the rain, and rust again, I would need the oil-can badly."

It was a bit of good luck to have their new comrade join the party, for soon after they had begun their journey again they came to a place where the trees and branches grew so thick over the road that the travellers could not pass. But the Tin Woodman set to work with his axe and chopped so well that soon he cleared a passage for the entire party.

Dorothy was thinking so earnestly as they walked along that she did not notice when the Scarecrow stumbled into a hole and rolled over to the side of the road. Indeed, he was obliged to call to her to help him up again.

"Why didn't you walk around the hole?" asked the Tin Woodman.

"I don't know enough," replied the Scarecrow, cheerfully. "My head is stuffed with straw, you know, and that is why I am going to Oz to ask him for some brains."

"Oh, I see," said the Tin Woodman. "But, after all, brains are not the best things in the world."

"Have you any?" enquired the Scarecrow.

"No, my head is quite empty," answered the Woodman; "but once I had brains, and a heart also; so, having tried them both, I should much rather have a heart."

"And why is that?" asked the Scarecrow.

"I will tell you my story, and then you will know."

So, while they were walking through the forest, the Tin Woodman told the following story:

"I was born the son of a woodman who chopped down trees in the forest and sold the wood for a living. When I grew up I too became a wood-chopper, and after my father died[7] I took care of my old mother as long as she lived. Then I made up my mind that instead of living alone, I would marry, so that I might not become lonely.

"There was one of the Munchkin girls who was so beautiful that I soon grew to love her with all my heart. She, on her part, promised to marry me as soon as I could earn enough money to build a better house for her; so I set to work harder than ever. But the girl lived with an old woman who did not want her to marry anyone, for she was so lazy she wished the girl to remain with her and do the cooking and the housework. So the old woman went to the Wicked Witch of the East, and promised her two sheep and a cow if she would prevent the marriage. Thereupon the Wicked Witch enchanted my axe, and when I was chopping away at my best one day, for I was anxious to get the new house and my wife as soon as possible, the axe slipped all at once and cut off my left leg.

"This at first seemed a great misfortune, for I knew a one-legged man could not do very well as a wood-chopper. So I went to a tin-smith and had him make me a new leg out of tin. The leg worked very well, once I was used to it; but my action angered the Wicked Witch of the East, for she had promised the old woman I should not marry the pretty Munchkin girl. When I began chopping again my axe slipped and cut off my right leg. Again I went to the tinner, and again he made me a leg out of tin. After this the enchanted axe cut off my arms, one after the other; but, nothing daunted, I had them replaced with tin ones. The Wicked Witch then made the axe slip and cut off my head, and at first I thought that was the end of me. But the tinner happened to come along, and he made me a new head out of tin.

"I thought I had beaten the Wicked Witch then, and I worked harder than ever; but I little knew how cruel my enemy could be. She thought of a new way to kill my love for the beautiful Munchkin maiden, and made my axe slip again, so that it cut right through my body, splitting me into two halves. Once more the tinner came to my help and made me a body of tin, fastening my tin arms and legs and head to it, by means of joints, so that I could move around as well as ever. But, alas! I had now no heart, so that I lost all my love for the Munchkin girl, and did not care whether I married her or not. I suppose she is still living with the old woman, waiting for me to come after her.

"My body shone so brightly in the sun that I felt very proud of it and it did not matter now if my axe slipped, for it could not cut me. There was only one danger—that my joints would rust; but I kept an oil-can in my cottage and took care to oil myself whenever I needed it. However, there came a day when I forgot to do this, and, being caught in a rainstorm, before I thought of the danger my joints had rusted, and I was left to stand in the woods until you came to help me. It was a terrible thing to undergo, but during the year I stood there I had time to think that the greatest loss I had known was the loss of my heart. While I was in love I was the happiest man on earth; but no one can love who has not a heart, and so I am resolved to ask Oz to give me one. If he does, I will go back to the Munchkin maiden and marry her."[8]

Both Dorothy and the Scarecrow had been greatly interested in the story of the Tin Woodman, and now they knew why he was so anxious to get a new heart.

"All the same," said the Scarecrow, "I shall ask for the brains instead of a heart; for a fool would not know what to do with a heart if he had one."

"I shall take the heart," returned the Tin Woodman; "for brains do not make one happy, and happiness is the best thing in the world."

Dorothy did not say anything, for she was puzzled to know which of her two friends was right, and she decided if she could only get back to Kansas and Aunt Em it did not matter so much whether the Woodman had no brains and the Scarecrow no heart, or each got what he wanted.

What worried her most was the bread was nearly gone, and another meal for herself and Toto would empty the basket. To be sure neither the Woodman nor the Scarecrow ever ate anything, but she was not made of tin nor straw, and could not live unless she was fed.

*"You ought to be ashamed of yourself!"*

· V I ·

# The Cowardly Lion

ALL this time Dorothy and her companions had been walking through the thick woods. The road was still paved with yellow brick, but these were much covered by dried branches and dead leaves from the trees, and the walking was not at all good.

There were few birds in this part of the forest, for birds love the open country where there is plenty of sunshine; but now and then there came a deep growl from some wild animal hidden among the trees. These sounds made the little girl's heart beat fast, for she did not know what made them; but Toto knew, and he walked close to Dorothy's side, and did not even bark in return.

"How long will it be," the child asked of the Tin Woodman, "before we are out of the forest?"

"I cannot tell," was the answer, "for I have never been to the Emerald City. But my father went there once, when I was a boy, and he said it was a long journey through a dangerous country, although nearer to the city where Oz dwells the country is beautiful. But I am not afraid so long as I have my oil-can, and nothing can hurt the Scarecrow, while you bear upon your forehead the mark of the good Witch's kiss, and that will protect you from harm."

"But Toto!" said the girl, anxiously; "what will protect him?"

"We must protect him ourselves, if he is in danger," replied the Tin Woodman.

Just as he spoke there came from the forest a terrible roar, and the next moment a great Lion bounded into the road. With one blow of his paw he sent the Scarecrow spinning over and over to the edge of the road, and then he struck at the Tin Woodman with his sharp claws. But, to the Lion's surprise, he could make no impression on the tin, although the Woodman fell over in the road and lay still.

Little Toto, now that he had an enemy to face, ran barking toward the Lion, and the great beast had opened his mouth to bite the dog, when Dorothy, fearing Toto would be killed, and heedless of danger, rushed forward and slapped the Lion upon his nose as hard as she could, while she cried out:

"Don't you dare to bite Toto! You ought to be ashamed of yourself, a big beast like you, to bite a poor little dog!"

"I didn't bite him," said the Lion, as he rubbed his nose with his paw where Dorothy had hit it.

"No, but you tried to," she retorted. "You are nothing but a big coward."

"I know it," said the Lion, hanging his head in shame; "I've always known it. But how can I help it?"

"I don't know, I'm sure. To think of your striking a stuffed man, like the poor Scarecrow!"

"Is he stuffed?" asked the Lion, in surprise, as he watched her pick up the Scarecrow and set him upon his feet, while she patted him into shape again.

"Of course he's stuffed," replied Dorothy, who was still angry.

"That's why he went over so easily," remarked the Lion. "It astonished me to see him whirl around so. Is the other one stuffed, also?"

"No," said Dorothy, "he's made of tin." And she helped the Woodman up again.

"That's why he nearly blunted my claws," said the Lion. "When they scratched against the tin it made a cold shiver run down my back. What is that little animal you are so tender of?"

"He is my dog, Toto," answered Dorothy.

"Is he made of tin, or stuffed?" asked the Lion.

"Neither. He's a—a—a meat dog," said the girl.

"Oh. He's a curious animal, and seems remarkably small, now that I look at him. No one would think of biting such a little thing except a coward like me," continued the Lion, sadly.

"What makes you a coward?" asked Dorothy, looking at the great beast in wonder, for he was as big as a small horse.

"It's a mystery," replied the Lion. "I suppose I was born that way. All the other animals in the forest naturally expect me to be brave, for the Lion is everywhere thought to be the King of Beasts.

# The Cowardly Lion

I learned that if I roared very loudly every living thing was frightened and got out of my way. Whenever I've met a man I've been awfully scared; but I just roared at him, and he has always run away as fast as he could go. If the elephants and the tigers and the bears had ever tried to fight me, I should have run myself—I'm such a coward; but just as soon as they hear me roar they all try to get away from me, and of course I let them go."

"But that isn't right. The King of Beasts shouldn't be a coward," said the Scarecrow.

"I know it," returned the Lion, wiping a tear from his eye with the tip of his tail; "it is my great sorrow, and makes my life very unhappy. But whenever there is danger my heart begins to beat fast."

"Perhaps you have heart disease," said the Tin Woodman.

"It may be," said the Lion.

"If you have," continued the Tin Woodman, "you ought to be glad, for it proves you have a heart. For my part, I have no heart; so I cannot have heart disease."

"Perhaps," said the Lion, thoughtfully, "if I had no heart I should not be a coward."

"Have you brains?" asked the Scarecrow.

"I suppose so. I've never looked to see," replied the Lion.

"I am going to the great Oz to ask him to give me some," remarked the Scarecrow, "for my head is stuffed with straw."

"And I am going to ask him to give me a heart," said the Woodman.

"And I am going to ask him to send Toto and me back to Kansas," added Dorothy.

"Do you think Oz could give me courage?" asked the Cowardly Lion.

"Just as easily as he could give me brains," said the Scarecrow.

"Or give me a heart," said the Tin Woodman.

"Or send me back to Kansas," said Dorothy.

"Then, if you don't mind, I'll go with you," said the Lion, "for my life is simply unbearable without a bit of courage."

"You will be very welcome," answered Dorothy, "for you will help to keep away the other wild beasts. It seems to me they must be more cowardly than you are if they allow you to scare them so easily."

"They really are," said the Lion; "but that doesn't make me any braver, and as long as I know myself to be a coward I shall be unhappy."

So once more the little company set off upon the journey, the Lion walking with stately strides at Dorothy's side. Toto did not approve this new comrade at first, for he could not forget how nearly he had been crushed between the Lion's great jaws; but after a time he became more at ease, and presently Toto and the Cowardly Lion had grown to be good friends.

During the rest of that day there was no other adventure to mar the peace of their journey. Once, indeed, the Tin Woodman stepped upon a beetle that was crawling along the road, and killed the poor little thing. This made the Tin Woodman very unhappy, for he was always careful not to hurt any living creature; and as he walked along he wept several tears of sorrow and regret. These tears ran slowly down his face and over the hinges of his jaw, and there they rusted. When Dorothy presently asked him a question the Tin Woodman could not open his mouth, for his jaws were tightly rusted together. He became greatly frightened at this and made many motions to Dorothy to relieve him, but she could not understand. The Lion was also puzzled to know what was wrong. But the Scarecrow seized the oil-can from Dorothy's basket and oiled the Woodman's jaws, so that after a few moments he could talk as well as before.

"This will serve me a lesson," said he, "to look where I step. For if I should kill another bug or beetle I should surely cry again, and crying rusts my jaw so that I cannot speak."

Thereafter he walked very carefully, with his eyes on the road, and when he saw a tiny ant toiling by he would step over it, so as not to harm it. The Tin Woodman knew very well he had no heart, and therefore he took great care never to be cruel or unkind to anything.

"You people with hearts," he said, "have something to guide you, and need never do wrong; but I have no heart, and so I must be very careful. When Oz gives me a heart of course I needn't mind so much."

# The Journey to the Great Oz

THEY were obliged to camp out that night under a large tree in the forest, for there were no houses near. The tree made a good, thick covering to protect them from the dew, and the Tin Woodman chopped a great pile of wood with his axe and Dorothy built a splendid fire that warmed her and made her feel less lonely. She and Toto ate the last of their bread, and now she did not know what they would do for breakfast.

"If you wish," said the Lion, "I will go into the forest and kill a deer for you. You can roast it by the fire, since your tastes are so peculiar that you prefer cooked food, and then you will have a very good breakfast."

"Don't! please don't," begged the Tin Woodman. "I should certainly weep if you killed a poor deer, and then my jaws would rust again."

But the Lion went away into the forest and found his own supper, and no one ever knew what it was, for he didn't mention it. And the Scarecrow found a tree full of nuts and filled Dorothy's basket with them, so that she would not be hungry for a long time. She thought this was very kind and thoughtful of the Scarecrow, but she laughed heartily at the awkward way in which the poor creature picked up the nuts. His padded hands were so clumsy and the nuts were so small that he dropped almost as many as he put in the basket. But the Scarecrow did not mind how long it took him to fill the basket, for it enabled him to keep away from the fire, as he feared a spark might get into his straw and burn him up. So he kept a good distance away from the flames, and only came near to cover Dorothy with dry leaves when she lay down to sleep. These kept her very snug and warm and she slept soundly until morning.

When it was daylight the girl bathed her face in a little rippling brook and soon after they all started toward the Emerald City.

This was to be an eventful day for the travellers. They had hardly been walking an hour when they saw before them a great ditch that crossed the road and divided the forest as far as they could see on either side. It was a very wide ditch, and when they crept up to the edge and looked into it they could see it was also very deep, and there were many big, jagged rocks at the bottom. The sides were so steep that none of them could climb down, and for a moment it seemed that their journey must end.

"What shall we do?" asked Dorothy, despairingly.

"I haven't the faintest idea," said the Tin Woodman; and the Lion shook his shaggy mane and looked thoughtful. But the Scarecrow said:

"We cannot fly, that is certain; neither can we climb down into this great ditch. Therefore, if we cannot jump over it, we must stop where we are."

"I think I could jump over it," said the Cowardly Lion, after measuring the distance carefully in his mind.

"Then we are all right," answered the Scarecrow; "for you can carry us all over on your back, one at a time."

"Well, I'll try it," said the Lion. "Who will go first?"

"I will," declared the Scarecrow; "for, if you found that you could not jump over the gulf, Dorothy would be killed, or the Tin Woodman badly dented on the rocks below. But if I am on your back it will not matter so much, for the fall would not hurt me at all."

"I am terribly afraid of falling, myself," said the Cowardly Lion, "but I suppose there is nothing to do but try it. So get on my back and we will make the attempt."

The Scarecrow sat upon the Lion's back, and the big beast walked to the edge of the gulf and crouched down.

"Why don't you run and jump?" asked the Scarecrow.

"Because that isn't the way we lions do these things," he replied. Then giving a great spring, he shot through the air and landed safely on the other side. They were all greatly pleased to see how easily he did it, and after the Scarecrow had got down from his back the Lion sprang across the ditch again.

Dorothy thought she would go next; so she took Toto in her arms and climbed on the Lion's back, holding tightly to his mane with one hand. The next moment it seemed as if she was flying through the air; and then, before she had time to think about it, she was safe on the other side. The Lion went back a third time and got the Tin Woodman, and then they all sat down and for a few moments to give the beast a chance to rest, for his great leaps had made his breath short, and he panted like a big dog that has been running too long.

They found the forest very thick on this side, and it looked dark and gloomy. After the Lion had rested they started along the road of yellow brick, silently wondering, each in his own mind, if ever they would come to the end of the woods and reach the bright sunshine again. To add to their discomfort, they soon heard strange noises in the depths of the forest, and the Lion whispered to them that it was in this part of the country that the Kalidahs lived.[9]

"What are the Kalidahs?" asked the girl.

"They are monstrous beasts with bodies like bears and heads like tigers," replied the Lion; "and with claws so long and sharp that they could tear me in two as easily as I could kill Toto. I'm terribly afraid of the Kalidahs."

"I'm not surprised that you are," returned Dorothy. "They must be dreadful beasts."

The Lion was about to reply when suddenly they came to another gulf across the road; but this one was so broad and deep that the Lion knew at once he could not leap across it.

So they sat down to consider what they should do, and after serious thought the Scarecrow said,

"Here is a great tree, standing close to the ditch. If the Tin Woodman can chop it down, so that it will fall to the other side, we can walk across it easily."

"That is a first rate idea," said the Lion. "One would almost suspect you had brains in your head, instead of straw."

The Woodman set to work at once, and so sharp was his axe that the tree was soon chopped nearly through. Then the Lion put his strong front legs against the tree and pushed with all his might, and slowly the big tree tipped and fell with a crash across the ditch, with its top branches on the other side.

They had just started to cross this queer bridge when a sharp growl made them all look up, and to their horror they saw running toward them two great beasts with bodies like bears and heads like tigers.

"They are the Kalidahs!" said the Cowardly Lion, beginning to tremble.

"Quick!" cried the Scarecrow, "let us cross over."

So Dorothy went first, holding Toto in her arms; the Tin Woodman followed, and the Scarecrow came next. The Lion, although he was certainly afraid, turned to face the Kalidahs, and then he gave so loud and terrible a roar that Dorothy screamed and the Scarecrow fell over backwards, while even the fierce beasts stopped short and looked at him in surprise.

But, seeing they were bigger than the Lion, and remembering that there were two of them and only one of him, the Kalidahs again rushed forward, and the Lion crossed over the tree and turned to see what they would do next. Without stopping an instant the fierce beasts also began to cross the tree, and the Lion said to Dorothy,

"We are lost, for they will surely tear us to pieces with their sharp claws. But stand close behind me, and I will fight them as long as I am alive."

"Wait a minute!" called the Scarecrow. He had been thinking what was best to be done, and now he asked the Woodman to chop away the end of the tree that rested on their side of the ditch. The Tin Woodman began to use his axe at once, and, just as the two Kalidahs were nearly across, the tree fell with a crash into the gulf, carrying the ugly, snarling brutes with it, and both were dashed to pieces on the sharp rocks at the bottom.

"Well," said the Cowardly Lion, drawing a long breath of relief, "I see we are going to live a little while longer, and I am glad of it, for it must be a very uncomfortable thing not to be alive. Those creatures frightened me so badly that my heart is beating yet."

"Ah," said the Tin Woodman, sadly, "I wish I had a heart to beat."

This adventure made the travellers more anxious than ever to get out of the forest, and they walked so fast that Dorothy became tired, and had to ride on the Lion's back. To their great joy the trees became thinner the further they advanced, and in the afternoon they suddenly came upon a broad river, flowing swiftly just before them. On the other side of the water they could see the road of yellow brick running through a beautiful country, with green meadows dotted with bright flowers and all the road bordered with trees hanging full of delicious fruits. They were greatly pleased to see this delightful country before them.

"How shall we cross the river?" asked Dorothy.

"That is easily done," replied the Scarecrow. "The Tin Woodman must build us a raft, so we can float to the other side."

So the Woodman took his axe and began to chop down small trees to make a raft, and while he was busy at this the Scarecrow found on the river bank a tree full of fine fruit. This pleased Dorothy, who had eaten nothing but nuts all day, and she made a hearty meal of the ripe fruit.

But it takes time to make a raft, even when one is as industrious and untiring as the Tin Woodman, and when night came the work was not done. So they found a cozy place under the trees where they slept well until the morning; and Dorothy dreamed of the Emerald City, and of the good Wizard Oz, who would soon send her back to her own home again.

# The Deadly Poppy Field

OUR little party of travellers awakened next morning refreshed and full of hope, and Dorothy breakfasted like a princess off peaches and plums from the trees beside the river.

Behind them was the dark forest they had passed safely through, although they had suffered many discouragements; but before them was a lovely, sunny country that seemed to beckon them on to the Emerald City.

To be sure, the broad river now cut them off from this beautiful land; but the raft was nearly done, and after the Tin Woodman had cut a few more logs and fastened them together with wooden pins, they were ready to start. Dorothy sat down in the middle of the raft and held Toto in her arms. When the Cowardly Lion stepped upon the raft it tipped badly, for he was big and heavy; but the Scarecrow and the Tin Woodman stood upon the other end to steady it, and they had long poles in their hands to push the raft through the water.

They got along quite well at first, but when they reached the middle of the river the swift current swept the raft down stream, farther and farther away from the road of yellow brick; and the water grew so deep that the long poles would not touch the bottom.

"This is bad," said the Tin Woodman, "for if we cannot get to the land we shall be carried into the country of the Wicked Witch of the West, and she will enchant us and make us her slaves."

"And then I should get no brains," said the Scarecrow.

"And I should get no courage," said the Cowardly Lion.

"And I should get no heart," said the Tin Woodman.

"And I should never get back to Kansas," said Dorothy.

"We must certainly get to the Emerald City if we can," the

Scarecrow continued, and he pushed so hard on his long pole that it stuck fast in the mud at the bottom of the river, and before he could pull it out again, or let go, the raft was swept away and the poor Scarecrow left clinging to the pole in the middle of the river.

"Good-bye!" he called after them, and they were very sorry to leave him; indeed, the Tin Woodman began to cry, but fortunately remembered that he might rust, and so dried his tears on Dorothy's apron.

Of course this was a bad thing for the Scarecrow.

"I am now worse off than when I first met Dorothy," he thought. "Then, I was stuck on a pole in a cornfield, where I could make believe scare the crows, at any rate; but surely there is no use for a Scarecrow stuck on a pole in the middle of a river. I am afraid I shall never have any brains, after all!"

Down the stream the raft floated, and the poor Scarecrow was left far behind. Then the Lion said:

"Something must be done to save us. I think I can swim to the shore and pull the raft after me, if you will only hold fast to the tip of my tail."

So he sprang into the water and the Tin Woodman caught fast hold of his tail, when the Lion began to swim with all his might toward the shore. It was hard work, although he was so big; but by and by they were drawn out of the current, and then Dorothy took the Tin Woodman's long pole and helped push the raft to the land.

They were all tired out when they reached the shore at last and stepped off upon the pretty green grass, and they also knew that the stream had carried them a long way past the road of yellow brick that led to the Emerald City.

"What shall we do now?" asked the Tin Woodman, as the Lion lay down on the grass to let the sun dry him.

"We must get back to the road, in some way," said Dorothy.

"The best plan will be to walk along the river bank until we come to the road again," remarked the Lion.

So when they were rested, Dorothy picked up her basket and they started along the grassy bank, back to the road from which the river had carried them. It was a lovely country, with plenty of flowers and fruit trees and sunshine to cheer them, and had they not felt so sorry for the poor Scarecrow they could have been very happy.

They walked along as fast as they could, Dorothy only stopping once to pick a beautiful flower; and after a time the Tin Woodman cried out,

"Look!"

Then they all looked at the river and saw the Scarecrow perched upon his pole in the middle of the water, looking very lonely and sad.

"What can we do to save him?" asked Dorothy.

The Lion and the Woodman both shook their heads, for they did not know. So they sat down upon the bank and gazed wistfully at the Scarecrow until a Stork flew by, which, seeing them, stopped to rest at the water's edge.

"Who are you, and where are you going?" asked the Stork.

"I am Dorothy," answered the girl; "and these are my friends, the Tin Woodman and the Cowardly Lion; and we are going to the Emerald City."

"This isn't the road," said the Stork, as she twisted her long neck and looked sharply at the queer party.

"I know it," returned Dorothy, "but we have lost the Scarecrow, and are wondering how we shall get him again."

"Where is he?" asked the Stork.

"Over there in the river," answered the girl.

"If he wasn't so big and heavy I would get him for you," remarked the Stork.

"He isn't heavy a bit," said Dorothy, eagerly, "for he is stuffed with straw; and if you will bring him back to us we shall thank you ever and ever so much."

"Well, I'll try," said the Stork; "but if I find he is too heavy to carry I shall have to drop him in the river again."

So the big bird flew into the air and over the water till she came to where the Scarecrow was perched upon his pole. Then the Stork with her great claws grabbed the Scarecrow by the arm and carried him up into the air and back to the bank, where Dorothy and the Lion and the Tin Woodman and Toto were sitting.

When the Scarecrow found himself among his friends again he was so happy that he hugged them all, even the Lion and Toto; and as they walked along he sang "Tol-de-ri-de-oh!" at every step, he felt so gay.

"I was afraid I should have to stay in the river forever," he said, "but the kind Stork saved me, and if I ever get any brains I shall find the Stork again and do it some kindness in return."

"That's all right," said the Stork, who was flying along beside them. "I always like to help anyone in trouble. But I must go now, for my babies are waiting in the nest for me. I hope you will find the Emerald City and that Oz will help you."

"Thank you," replied Dorothy, and then the kind Stork flew into the air and was soon out of sight.

They walked along listening to the singing of the bright-colored birds and looking at the lovely flowers which now became so thick that the ground was carpeted with them. There were big yellow and white and blue and purple blossoms, besides great clusters of scarlet poppies, which were so brilliant in color they almost dazzled Dorothy's eyes.[10]

"Aren't they beautiful?" the girl asked, as she breathed in the spicy scent of the flowers.

"I suppose so," answered the Scarecrow. "When I have brains I shall probably like them better."

"If I only had a heart I should love them," added the Tin Woodman.

"I always did like flowers," said the Lion; "they seem so helpless and frail. But there are none in the forest so bright as these."

They now came upon more and more of the big scarlet poppies, and fewer and fewer of the other flowers; and soon they found themselves in the midst of a great meadow of poppies. Now it is well known that when there are many of these flowers together their odor is so powerful that anyone who breathes it falls asleep, and if the sleeper is not carried away from the scent of the flowers he sleeps on and on forever. But Dorothy did not know this, nor could she get away from the bright red flowers that were everywhere about; so presently her eyes grew heavy and she felt she must sit down to rest and to sleep.

## The Deadly Poppy Field

But the Tin Woodman would not let her do this.

"We must hurry and get back to the road of yellow brick before dark," he said; and the Scarecrow agreed with him. So they kept walking until Dorothy could stand no longer. Her eyes closed in spite of herself and she forgot where she was and fell among the poppies, fast asleep.

"What shall we do?" asked the Tin Woodman.

"If we leave her here she will die," said the Lion. "The smell of the flowers is killing us all. I myself can scarcely keep my eyes open and the dog is asleep already."

It was true; Toto had fallen down beside his little mistress. But the Scarecrow and the Tin Woodman, not being made of flesh, were not troubled by the scent of the flowers.

"Run fast," said the Scarecrow to the Lion, "and get out of this deadly flower-bed as soon as you can. We will bring the little girl with us, but if you should fall asleep you are too big to be carried."

So the Lion aroused himself and bounded forward as fast as he could go. In a moment he was out of sight.

"Let us make a chair with our hands, and carry her," said the Scarecrow. So they picked up Toto and put the dog in Dorothy's lap, and then they made a chair with their hands for the seat and their arms for the arms and carried the sleeping girl between them through the flowers.

On and on they walked, and it seemed that the great carpet of deadly flowers that surrounded them would never end. They followed the bend of the river, and at last came upon their friend the Lion, lying fast asleep among the poppies. The flowers had been too strong for the huge beast and he had given up, at last, and fallen only a short distance from the end of the poppy-bed, where the sweet grass spread in beautiful green fields before them.

"We can do nothing for him," said the Tin Woodman, sadly; "for he is much too heavy to lift. We must leave him here to sleep on forever, and perhaps he will dream that he has found courage at last."

"I'm sorry," said the Scarecrow; "the Lion was a very good comrade for one so cowardly. But let us go on."

They carried the sleeping girl to a pretty spot beside the river, far enough from the poppy field to prevent her breathing any more of the poison of the flowers, and here they laid her gently on the soft grass and waited for the fresh breeze to waken her.

# The Queen of the Field-Mice

WE CANNOT be far from the road of yellow brick, now," remarked the Scarecrow, as he stood beside the girl, "for we have come nearly as far as the river carried us away."

The Tin Woodman was about to reply when he heard a low growl, and turning his head (which worked beautifully on hinges) he saw a strange beast come bounding over the grass toward them. It was, indeed, a great, yellow wildcat, and the Woodman thought it must be chasing something, for its ears were lying close to its head and its mouth was wide open, showing two rows of ugly teeth, while its red eyes glowed like balls of fire. As it came nearer the Tin Woodman saw that running before the beast was a little gray field-mouse, and although he had no heart he knew it was wrong for the wildcat to kill such a pretty, harmless creature.

So the Woodman raised his axe, and as the wildcat ran by he gave it a quick blow that cut the beast's head clean off from its body, and it rolled over at his feet in two pieces.

The field-mouse, now that it was freed from its enemy, stopped short; and coming slowly up to the Woodman it said, in a squeaky little voice,

"Oh, thank you! Thank you ever so much for saving my life."

"Don't speak of it, I beg of you," replied the Woodman. "I have no heart, you know, so I am careful to help all those who may need a friend, even if it happens to be only a mouse."

"Only a mouse!" cried the little animal, indignantly; "why, I am a Queen—the Queen of all the field-mice!"

"Oh, indeed," said the Woodman, making a bow.

"Therefore you have done a great deed, as well as a brave one, in saving my life," added the Queen.

At that moment several mice were seen running up as fast as

their little legs could carry them, and when they saw their Queen they exclaimed,

"Oh, your Majesty, we thought you would be killed! How did you manage to escape the great Wildcat?" and they all bowed so low to the little Queen that they almost stood upon their heads.

"This funny tin man," she answered, "killed the Wildcat and saved my life. So hereafter you must all serve him, and obey his slightest wish."

"We will!" cried all the mice, in a shrill chorus. And then they scampered in all directions, for Toto had awakened from his sleep, and seeing all these mice around him he gave one bark of delight and jumped right into the middle of the group. Toto had always loved to chase mice when he lived in Kansas, and he saw no harm in it.

But the Tin Woodman caught the dog in his arms and held him tight, while he called to the mice: "Come back! come back! Toto shall not hurt you."

At this the Queen of the Mice stuck her head out from a clump of grass and asked, in a timid voice,

"Are you sure he will not bite us?"

"I will not let him," said the Woodman; "so do not be afraid."

One by one the mice came creeping back, and Toto did not bark again, although he tried to get out of the Woodman's arms, and would have bitten him had he not known very well he was made of tin. Finally one of the biggest mice spoke.

"Is there anything we can do," it asked, "to repay you for saving the life of our Queen?"

"Nothing that I know of," answered the Woodman; but the Scarecrow, who had been trying to think, but could not because his head was stuffed with straw, said, quickly,

"Oh, yes; you can save our friend, the Cowardly Lion, who is asleep in the poppy bed."

"A Lion!" cried the little Queen; "why, he would eat us all up."

"Oh, no," declared the Scarecrow; "this Lion is a coward."

"Really?" asked the Mouse.

"He says so himself," answered the Scarecrow, "and he would

never hurt anyone who is our friend. If you will help us to save him I promise that he shall treat you all with kindness."

"Very well," said the Queen, "we will trust you. But what shall we do?"

"Are there many of these mice which call you Queen and are willing to obey you?"

"Oh, yes; there are thousands," she replied.

"Then send for them all to come here as soon as possible, and let each one bring a long piece of string."

The Queen turned to the mice that attended her and told them to go at once and get all her people. As soon as they heard her orders they ran away in every direction as fast as possible.

"Now," said the Scarecrow to the Tin Woodman, "you must go to those trees by the river-side and make a truck that will carry the Lion."

So the Woodman went at once to the trees and began to work; and he soon made a truck out of the limbs of trees, from which he chopped away all the leaves and branches. He fastened it together with wooden pegs and made the four wheels out of short pieces of a big tree-trunk. So fast and so well did he work that by the time the mice began to arrive the truck was all ready for them.

They came from all directions, and there were thousands of them: big mice and little mice and middle-sized mice; and each one brought a piece of string in his mouth. It was about this time that Dorothy woke from her long sleep and opened her eyes. She was greatly astonished to find herself lying upon the grass, with thousands of mice standing around and looking at her timidly. But the Scarecrow told her about everything, and turning to the dignified little Mouse, he said,

"Permit me to introduce to you her Majesty, the Queen."

Dorothy nodded gravely and the Queen made a courtesy, after which she became quite friendly with the little girl.

The Scarecrow and the Woodman now began to fasten the mice to the truck, using the strings they had brought. One end of a string was tied around the neck of each mouse and the other end to the truck. Of course the truck was a thousand times bigger than any of the mice who were to draw it; but when all the mice had been harnessed they were able to pull it quite easily. Even the Scarecrow and the Tin Woodman could sit on it, and were drawn swiftly by their queer little horses to the place where the Lion lay asleep.

After a great deal of hard work, for the Lion was heavy, they managed to get him up on the truck. Then the Queen hurriedly gave her people the order to start, for she feared if the mice stayed among the poppies too long they also would fall asleep.

At first the little creatures, many though they were, could hardly stir the heavily loaded truck; but the Woodman and the Scarecrow both pushed from behind, and they got along better. Soon they rolled the Lion out of the poppy bed to the green fields, where he could breathe the sweet, fresh air again, instead of the poisonous scent of the flowers.

Dorothy came to meet them and thanked the little mice warmly for saving her companion from death. She had grown so fond of the big Lion she was glad he had been rescued.

Then the mice were unharnessed from the truck and scampered away through the grass to their homes. The Queen of the Mice was the last to leave.

"If ever you need us again," she said, "come out into the field and call, and we shall hear you and come to your assistance. Good-bye!"

"Good-bye!" they all answered, and away the Queen ran, while Dorothy held Toto tightly lest he should run after her and frighten her.

After this they sat down beside the Lion until he should awaken; and the Scarecrow brought Dorothy some fruit from a tree near by, which she ate for her dinner.

*"The Lion ate some of the porridge."*

# The Guardian of the Gates

IT WAS some time before the Cowardly Lion awakened, for he had lain among the poppies a long while, breathing in their deadly fragrance; but when he did open his eyes and roll off the truck he was very glad to find himself still alive.

"I ran fast as I could," he said, sitting down and yawning; "but the flowers were too strong for me. How did you get me out?"

Then they told him of the field-mice, and how they had generously saved him from death; and the Cowardly Lion laughed, and said,

"I have always thought myself very big and terrible; yet such small things as flowers came near to killing me, and such small animals as mice have saved my life. How strange it all is! But, comrades, what shall we do now?"

"We must journey on until we find the road of yellow brick again," said Dorothy; "and then we can keep on to the Emerald City."

So, the Lion being fully refreshed, and feeling quite himself again, they all started upon the journey, greatly enjoying the walk through the soft, fresh grass; and it was not long before they reached the road of yellow brick and turned again toward the Emerald City where the great Oz dwelt.

The road was smooth and well paved, now, and the country about was beautiful; so that the travellers rejoiced in leaving the forest far behind, and with it the many dangers they had met in its gloomy shades. Once more they could see fences built beside the road; but these were painted green, and when they came to a small house, in which a farmer evidently lived, that also was painted green. They passed by several of these houses during the afternoon, and sometimes people came to the doors and looked at them as if they would like to ask questions, but no one came near them nor spoke to them because of the great Lion, of which they were much afraid. The people were all dressed in clothing of a lovely emerald green color and wore peaked hats like those of the Munchkins.

"This must be the Land of Oz," said Dorothy, "and we are surely getting near the Emerald City."

"Yes," answered the Scarecrow; "everything is green here, while in the country of the Munchkins blue was the favorite color. But the people do not seem to be as friendly as the Munchkins and I'm afraid we shall be unable to find a place to pass the night."

"I should like something to eat besides fruit," said the girl, "and I'm sure Toto is nearly starved. Let us stop at the next house and talk to the people."

So, when they came to a good sized farm house, Dorothy walked boldly up to the door and knocked. A woman opened it just far enough to look out, and said,

"What do you want, child, and why is that great Lion with you?"

"We wish to pass the night with you, if you will allow us," answered Dorothy; "and the Lion is my friend and comrade, and would not hurt you for the world."

"Is he tame?" asked the woman, opening the door a little wider.

"Oh, yes," said the girl, "and he is a great coward, too; so that he will be more afraid of you than you are of him."

"Well," said the woman, after thinking it over and taking another peep at the Lion, "if that is the case you may come in, and I will give you some supper and a place to sleep."

So they all entered the house, where there were, besides the woman, two children and a man. The man had hurt his leg, and was lying on the couch in a corner. They seemed greatly surprised to see so strange a company, and while the woman was busy laying the table the man asked,

"Where are you all going?"

"To the Emerald City," said Dorothy, "to see the great Oz."

"Oh, indeed!" exclaimed the man. "Are you sure that Oz will see you?"

"Why not?" she replied.

## The Guardian of the Gates

"Why, it is said that he never lets any one come into his presence. I have been to the Emerald City many times, and it is a beautiful and wonderful place; but I have never been permitted to see the great Oz, nor do I know of any living person who has seen him."

"Does he never go out?" asked the Scarecrow.

"Never. He sits day after day in the great throne room of his palace, and even those who wait upon him do not see him face to face."

"What is he like?" asked the girl.

"That is hard to tell," said the man, thoughtfully. "You see, Oz is a Great Wizard, and can take on any form he wishes. So that some say he looks like a bird; and some say he looks like an elephant; and some say he looks like a cat. To others he appears as a beautiful fairy, or a brownie, or in any other form that pleases him. But who the real Oz is, when he is in his own form, no living person can tell."

"That is very strange," said Dorothy; "but we must try, in some way, to see him, or we shall have made our journey for nothing."

"Why do you wish to see the terrible Oz?" asked the man.

"I want him to give me some brains," said the Scarecrow, eagerly.

"Oh, Oz could do that easily enough," declared the man. "He has more brains than he needs."

"And I want him to give me a heart," said the Tin Woodman.

"That will not trouble him," continued the man, "for Oz has a large collection of hearts, of all sizes and shapes."

"And I want him to give me courage," said the Cowardly Lion.

"Oz keeps a great pot of courage in his throne room," said the man, "which he has covered with a golden plate, to keep it from running over. He will be glad to give you some."

"And I want him to send me back to Kansas," said Dorothy.

"Where is Kansas?" asked the man, in surprise.

"I don't know," replied Dorothy, sorrowfully; "but it is my home, and I'm sure it's somewhere."

"Very likely. Well, Oz can do anything; so I suppose he will find Kansas for you. But first you must get to see him, and that will be a hard task; for the Great Wizard does not like to see anyone, and he usually has his own way. But what do YOU want?" he continued, speaking to Toto. Toto only wagged his tail; for, strange to say, he could not speak.[11]

The woman now called to them that supper was ready, so they gathered around the table and Dorothy ate some delicious porridge and a dish of scrambled eggs and a plate of nice white bread, and enjoyed her meal. The Lion ate some of the porridge, but did not care for it, saying it was made from oats and oats were food for horses, not for lions. The Scarecrow and the Tin Woodman ate nothing at all. Toto ate a little of everything, and was glad to get a good supper again.

The woman now gave Dorothy a bed to sleep in, and Toto lay down beside her, while the Lion guarded the door of her room so she might not be disturbed. The Scarecrow and the Tin Wood-man stood up in a corner and kept quiet all night, although of course they could not sleep.

The next morning, as soon as the sun was up, they started on their way, and soon saw a beautiful green glow in the sky just be-fore them.

"That must be the Emerald City," said Dorothy.

As they walked on, the green glow became brighter and brighter, and it seemed that at last they were nearing the end of their travels. Yet it was afternoon before they came to the great wall that sur-rounded the city. It was high and thick, and of a bright green color.

In front of them, and at the end of the road of yellow brick, was a big gate, all studded with emeralds that glittered so in the sun that even the painted eyes of the Scarecrow were dazzled by their brilliancy.

There was a bell beside the gate, and Dorothy pushed the button and heard a silvery tinkle sound within. Then the big gate swung slowly open, and they all passed through and found themselves in a high arched room, the walls of which glistened with countless emeralds.

Before them stood a little man about the same size as the Munch-kins. He was clothed all in green, from his head to his feet, and even his skin was of a greenish tint. At his side was a large green box.

When he saw Dorothy and her companions the man asked,

"What do you wish in the Emerald City?"

"We came here to see the Great Oz," said Dorothy.

The man was so surprised at this answer that he sat down to think it over.

"It has been many years since anyone asked me to see Oz," he said, shaking his head in perplexity. "He is powerful and terrible, and if you come on an idle or foolish errand to bother the wise reflections of the Great Wizard, he might be angry and destroy you all in an instant."

"But it is not a foolish errand, nor an idle one," replied the Scarecrow; "it is important. And we have been told that Oz is a good Wizard."

"So he is," said the green man; "and he rules the Emerald City wisely and well. But to those who are not honest, or who approach him from curiosity, he is most terrible, and few have ever dared ask to see his face. I am the Guardian of the Gates, and since you demand to see the Great Oz I must take you to his palace. But first you must put on the spectacles."

"Why?" asked Dorothy.

"Because if you did not wear spectacles the brightness and glory of the Emerald City would blind you. Even those who live in the City must wear spectacles night and day. They are all locked on, for Oz so ordered it when the City was first built, and I have the only key that will unlock them."

He opened the big box, and Dorothy saw that it was filled with spectacles of every size and shape. All of them had green glasses in them. The Guardian of the Gates found a pair that would just fit Dorothy and put them over her eyes. There were two golden bands fastened to them that passed around the back of her head, where they were locked together by a little key that was at the end of a chain the Guardian of the Gates wore around his neck. When they were on, Dorothy could not take them off had she wished, but of course she did not want to be blinded by the glare of the Emerald City, so she said nothing.

Then the green man fitted spectacles for the Scarecrow and the Tin Woodman and the Lion, and even on little Toto; and all were locked fast with the key.

Then the Guardian of the Gates put on his own glasses and told them he was ready to show them to the palace. Taking a big golden key from a peg on the wall he opened another gate, and they all followed him through the portal into the streets of the Emerald City.

*"The Eyes looked at her thoughtfully."*

# The Wonderful Emerald City of Oz

E VEN with eyes protected by the green spectacles Dorothy and her friends were at first dazzled by the brilliancy of the wonderful City. The streets were lined with beautiful houses all built of green marble and studded everywhere with sparkling emeralds. They walked over a pavement of the same green marble, and where the blocks were joined together were rows of emeralds, set closely, and glittering in the brightness of the sun. The window panes were of green glass; even the sky above the City had a green tint, and the rays of the sun were green.

There were many people, men, women and children, walking about, and these were all dressed in green clothes and had greenish skins. They looked at Dorothy and her strangely assorted company with wondering eyes, and the children all ran away and hid behind their mothers when they saw the Lion; but no one spoke to them. Many shops stood in the street, and Dorothy saw that everything in them was green. Green candy and green pop-corn were offered for sale, as well as green shoes, green hats and green clothes of all sorts. At one place a man was selling green lemonade, and when the children bought it Dorothy could see that they paid for it with green pennies.[12]

There seemed to be no horses nor animals of any kind; the men carried things around in little green carts, which they pushed before them. Everyone seemed happy and contented and prosperous.

The Guardian of the Gates led them through the streets until they came to a big building, exactly in the middle of the city, which was the Palace of Oz, the Great Wizard. There was a soldier before the door, dressed in a green uniform and wearing a long green beard.

"Here are strangers," said the Guardian of the Gates to him, "and they demand to see the Great Oz."

"Step inside," answered the soldier, "and I will carry your message to him."

So they passed through the Palace gates and were led into a big room with a green carpet and lovely green furniture set with emeralds. The soldier made them all wipe their feet upon a green mat before entering this room, and when they were seated he said, politely,

"Please make yourselves comfortable while I go to the door of the Throne Room and tell Oz you are here."

They had to wait a long time before the soldier returned. When, at last, he came back, Dorothy asked,

"Have you seen Oz?"

"Oh, no," returned the soldier; "I have never seen him. But I spoke to him as he sat behind his screen, and gave him your message. He says he will grant you an audience, if you so desire; but each one of you must enter his presence alone, and he will admit but one each day. Therefore, as you must remain in the Palace for several days, I will have you shown to rooms where you may rest in comfort after your journey."

"Thank you," replied the girl; "that is very kind of Oz."

The soldier now blew upon a green whistle, and at once a young girl,[13] dressed in a pretty green silk gown, entered the room. She had lovely green hair and green eyes, and she bowed low before Dorothy as she said,

"Follow me and I will show you your room."

So Dorothy said good-bye to all her friends except Toto, and taking the dog in her arms followed the green girl through seven passages and up three flights of stairs until they came to a room at the front of the Palace. It was the sweetest little room in the world, with a soft, comfortable bed that had sheets of green silk and a green velvet counterpane. There was a tiny fountain in the middle of the room, that shot a spray of green perfume into the air, to fall back into a beautifully carved green marble basin. Beautiful green flowers stood in the windows, and there was a shelf with a row of little green books. When Dorothy had time to open these books she found them full of queer green pictures that made her laugh, they were so funny.

In a wardrobe were many green dresses, made of silk and satin and velvet; and all of them fitted Dorothy exactly.

"Make yourself perfectly at home," said the green girl, "and if you wish for anything ring the bell. Oz will send for you to-morrow morning."

She left Dorothy alone and went back to the others. These she also led to rooms, and each one of them found himself lodged in a very pleasant part of the Palace. Of course this politeness was wasted on the Scarecrow; for when he found himself alone in his room he stood stupidly in one spot, just within the door-way, to wait till morning. It would not rest him to lie down, and he could not close his eyes; so he remained all night staring at a little spider which was weaving its web in a corner of the room, just as if it were not one of the most wonderful rooms in the world. The Tin Woodman lay down on his bed from force of habit, for he remembered when he was made of flesh; but not being able to sleep he passed the night moving his joints up and down to make sure they kept in good working order. The Lion would have preferred a bed of dried leaves in the forest, and did not like being shut up in a room; but he had too much sense to let this worry him, so he sprang upon the bed and rolled himself up like a cat and purred himself asleep in a minute.

The next morning, after breakfast, the green maiden came to fetch Dorothy, and she dressed her in one of the prettiest gowns—made of green brocaded satin. Dorothy put on a green silk apron and tied a green ribbon around Toto's neck, and they started for the Throne Room of the Great Oz.

First they came to a great hall in which were many ladies and gentlemen of the court, all dressed in rich costumes. These people had nothing to do but talk to each other, but they always came to wait outside the Throne Room every morning, although they were never permitted to see Oz. As Dorothy entered they looked at her curiously, and one of them whispered,

"Are you really going to look upon the face of Oz the Terrible?"

"Of course," answered the girl, "if he will see me."

"Oh, he will see you," said the soldier who had taken her message to the Wizard, "although he does not like to have people ask to see him. Indeed, at first he was angry, and said I should send you back where you came from. Then he asked me what you looked like, and when I mentioned your silver shoes he was very much interested. At last I told him about the mark upon your forehead, and he decided he would admit you to his presence."

Just then a bell rang, and the green girl said to Dorothy,

"That is the signal. You must go into the Throne Room alone."

She opened a little door and Dorothy walked boldly through and found herself in a wonderful place. It was a big, round room with a high arched roof, and the walls and ceiling and floor were covered with large emeralds set closely together. In the center of the roof was a great light, as bright as the sun, which made the emeralds sparkle in a wonderful manner.

But what interested Dorothy most was the big throne of green marble that stood in the middle of the room. It was shaped like a chair and sparkled with gems, as did everything else. In the center of the chair was an enormous Head, without body to support it or any arms or legs whatever. There was no hair upon this head, but it had eyes and nose and mouth, and was bigger than the head of the biggest giant.

As Dorothy gazed upon this in wonder and fear the eyes turned slowly and looked at her sharply and steadily. Then the mouth moved, and Dorothy heard a voice say:

"I am Oz, the Great and Terrible. Who are you, and why do you seek me?"

It was not such an awful voice as she had expected to come from the big Head; so she took courage and answered,

"I am Dorothy, the Small and Meek. I have come to you for help."

The eyes looked at her thoughtfully for a full minute. Then said the voice:

"Where did you get the silver shoes?"

"I got them from the Wicked Witch of the East, when my house fell on her and killed her," she replied.

"Where did you get the mark upon your forehead?" continued the voice.

"That is where the good Witch of the North kissed me when she bade me good-bye and sent me to you," said the girl.

Again the eyes looked at her sharply, and they saw she was telling the truth. Then Oz asked,

"What do you wish me to do?"

"Send me back to Kansas, where my Aunt Em and Uncle Henry are," she answered, earnestly. "I don't like your country, although it is so beautiful. And I am sure Aunt Em will be dreadfully worried over my being away so long."

The eyes winked three times, and then they turned up to the ceiling and down to the floor and rolled around so queerly that they seemed to see every part of the room. And at last they looked at Dorothy again.

"Why should I do this for you?" asked Oz.

"Because you are strong and I am weak; because you are a Great Wizard and I am only a helpless little girl," she answered.

"But you were strong enough to kill the Wicked Witch of the East," said Oz.

"That just happened," returned Dorothy, simply; "I could not help it."

"Well," said the Head, "I will give you my answer. You have no right to expect me to send you back to Kansas unless you do something for me in return. In this country everyone must pay for everything he gets. If you wish me to use my magic power to to send you home again you must do something for me first. Help me and I will help you."

"What must I do?" asked the girl.

"Kill the Wicked Witch of the West," answered Oz.

"But I cannot!" exclaimed Dorothy, greatly surprised.

"You killed the Witch of the East and you wear the silver shoes, which bear a powerful charm. There is now but one Wicked

Witch left in all this land, and when you can tell me she is dead I will send you back to Kansas—but not before."

The little girl began to weep, she was so much disappointed; and the eyes winked again and looked upon her anxiously, as if the Great Oz felt that she could help him if she would.

"I never killed anything, willingly," she sobbed; "and even if I wanted to, how could I kill the Wicked Witch? If you, who are Great and Terrible, cannot kill her yourself, how do you expect me to do it?"

"I do not know," said the Head; "but that is my answer, and until the Wicked Witch dies you will not see your Uncle and Aunt again. Remember that the Witch is Wicked—tremendously Wicked—and ought to be killed. Now go, and do not ask to see me again until you have done your task."

Sorrowfully Dorothy left the Throne Room and went back where the Lion and the Scarecrow and the Tin Woodman were waiting to hear what Oz had said to her.

"There is no hope for me," she said, sadly, "for Oz will not send me home until I have killed the Wicked Witch of the West; and that I can never do."

Her friends were sorry, but could do nothing to help her; so she went to her own room and lay down on the bed and cried herself to sleep.

The next morning the soldier with the green whiskers came to the Scarecrow and said,

"Come with me, for Oz has sent for you."

So the Scarecrow followed him and was admitted into the great Throne Room, where he saw, sitting in the emerald throne, a most lovely lady. She was dressed in green silk gauze and wore upon her flowing green locks a crown of jewels. Growing from her shoulders were wings, gorgeous in color and so light that they fluttered if the slightest breath of air reached them.

When the Scarecrow had bowed, as prettily as his straw stuffing would let him, before this beautiful creature, she looked upon him sweetly, and said,

"I am Oz, the Great and Terrible. Who are you, and why do you seek me?"

Now the Scarecrow, who had expected to see the great Head Dorothy had told him of, was much astonished; but he answered her bravely.

"I am only a Scarecrow, stuffed with straw. Therefore I have no brains, and I come to you praying that you will put brains in my head instead of straw, so that I may become as much a man as any other in your dominions."

"Why should I do this for you?" asked the lady.

"Because you are wise and powerful, and no one else can help me," answered the Scarecrow.

"I never grant favors without some return," said Oz; "but this much I will promise. If you will kill for me the Wicked Witch of the West I will bestow upon you a great many brains, and such good brains that you will be the wisest man in all the Land of Oz."

"I thought you asked Dorothy to kill the Witch," said the Scarecrow in surprise.

"So I did. I don't care who kills her. But until she is dead I will not grant your wish. Now go, and do not seek me again until you have earned the brains you so greatly desire."

The Scarecrow went sorrowfully back to his friends and told them what Oz had said; and Dorothy was surprised to find that the Great Wizard was not a Head, as she had seen him, but a lovely lady.

"All the same," said the Scarecrow, "she needs a heart as much as the Tin Woodman."

On the next morning the soldier with the green whiskers came to the Tin Woodman and said,

"Oz has sent for you. Follow me."

So the Tin Woodman followed him and came to the great Throne Room. He did not know whether he would find Oz a lovely lady or a Head, but he hoped it would be the lovely lady. "For," he said to himself, "if it is the Head, I am sure I shall not be given a heart, since a head has no heart of its own and therefore cannot feel for me. But if it is the lovely lady I shall beg hard for a heart, for all ladies are themselves said to be kindly hearted."

But when the Woodman entered the great Throne Room he saw neither the Head nor the Lady, for Oz had taken the shape of a most terrible Beast. It was nearly as big as an elephant, and the green throne seemed hardly strong enough to hold its weight. The Beast had a head like that of a rhinoceros, only there were five eyes in its face. There were five long arms growing out of its body and it also had five long, slim legs. Thick, woolly hair covered every part of it, and a more dreadful looking monster could not be imagined. It was fortunate the Tin Woodman had no heart at that moment, for it would have beat loud and fast from terror. But being only tin, the Woodman was not at all afraid, although he was much disappointed.

"I am Oz, the Great and Terrible," spake the Beast, in a voice that was one great roar. "Who are you, and why do you seek me?"

"I am a Woodman, and made of tin. Therefore I have no heart, and cannot love. I pray you to give me a heart that I may be as other men are."

"Why should I do this?" demanded the Beast.

"Because I ask it, and you alone can grant my request," answered the Woodman.

Oz gave a low growl at this, but said, gruffly,

"If you indeed desire a heart, you must earn it."

"How?" asked the Woodman.

"Help Dorothy to kill the Wicked Witch of the West," replied the Beast. "When the Witch is dead, come to me, and I then will give you the biggest and kindest and most loving heart in all the Land of Oz."[14]

So the Tin Woodman was forced to return sorrowfully to his friends and tell them of the terrible Beast he had seen. They all wondered greatly at the many forms the Great Wizard could take upon himself, and the Lion said,

"If he is a beast when I go to see him, I shall roar my loudest, and so frighten him that he will grant all I ask. And if he is the lovely lady, I shall pretend to spring upon her, and so compel her to do my bidding. And if he is the great Head, he will be at my mercy; for I will roll this head all about the room until he promises to give us what we desire. So be of good cheer my friends, for all will yet be well."

The next morning the soldier with the green whiskers led the

Lion to the great Throne Room and bade him enter the presence of Oz.

The Lion at once passed through the door, and glancing around saw, to his surprise, that before the throne was a Ball of Fire, so fierce and glowing he could scarcely bear to gaze upon it. His first thought was that Oz had by accident caught on fire and was burning up; but, when he tried to go nearer, the heat was so intense that it singed his whiskers, and he crept back tremblingly to a spot nearer the door.

Then a low, quiet voice came from the Ball of Fire, and these were the words it spoke:

"I am Oz, the Great and Terrible. Who are you, and why do you seek me?"

And the Lion answered, "I am a Cowardly Lion, afraid of everything. I come to you to beg that you give me courage, so that in reality I may become the King of Beasts, as men call me."

"Why should I give you courage?" demanded Oz.

"Because of all Wizards you are the greatest, and alone have power to grant my request," answered the Lion.

The Ball of Fire burned fiercely for a time, and the voice said, "Bring me proof that the Wicked Witch is dead, and that moment I will give you courage. But so long as the Witch lives you must remain a coward."

The Lion was angry at this speech, but could say nothing in reply, and while he stood silently gazing at the Ball of Fire it became so furiously hot that he turned tail and rushed from the room. He was glad to find his friends waiting for him, and told them of his terrible interview with the Wizard.

"What shall we do now?" asked Dorothy, sadly.

"There is only one thing we can do," returned the Lion, "and that is to go to the land of the Winkies, seek out the Wicked Witch, and destroy her."

"But suppose we cannot?" said the girl.

"Then I shall never have courage," declared the Lion.

"And I shall never have brains," added the Scarecrow.

"And I shall never have a heart," spoke the Tin Woodman.

"And I shall never see Aunt Em and Uncle Henry," said Dorothy, beginning to cry.

"Be careful!" cried the green girl, "the tears will fall on your green silk gown, and spot it."

So Dorothy dried her eyes and said,

"I suppose we must try it; but I am sure I do not want to kill anybody, even to see Aunt Em again."

"I will go with you; but I'm too much of a coward to kill the Witch," said the Lion.

"I will go too," declared the Scarecrow; "but I shall not be of much help to you, I am such a fool."

"I haven't the heart to harm even a Witch," remarked the Tin Woodman; "but if you go I certainly shall go with you."

Therefore it was decided to start upon their journey the next morning, and the Woodman sharpened his axe on a green grindstone and had all his joints properly oiled. The Scarecrow stuffed himself with fresh straw and Dorothy put new paint on his eyes that he might see better. The green girl, who was very kind to them, filled Dorothy's basket with good things to eat, and fastened a little bell around Toto's neck with a green ribbon.

They went to bed quite early and slept soundly until daylight, when they were awakened by the crowing of a green cock that lived in the back yard of the palace, and the cackling of a hen that had laid a green egg.

## · XII ·

# The Search for the Wicked Witch

THE soldier with the green whiskers led them through the streets of the Emerald City until they reached the room where the Guardian of the Gates lived. This officer unlocked their spectacles to put them back in his great box, and then he politely opened the gate for our friends.

"Which road leads to the Wicked Witch of the West?" asked Dorothy.

"There is no road," answered the Guardian of the Gates; "no one ever wishes to go that way."

"How, then, are we to find her?" enquired the girl.

"That will be easy," replied the man; "for when she knows you are in the Country of the Winkies she will find you, and make you all her slaves."

"Perhaps not," said the Scarecrow, "for we mean to destroy her."

"Oh, that is different," said the Guardian of the Gates. "No one has ever destroyed her before, so I naturally thought she would make slaves of you, as she has of all the rest. But take care; for she is wicked and fierce, and may not allow you to destroy her. Keep to the West, where the sun sets, and you cannot fail to find her."

They thanked him and bade him good-bye, and turned toward the West, walking over fields of soft grass dotted here and there with daisies and buttercups. Dorothy still wore the pretty silk dress she had put on in the palace, but now, to her surprise, she found it was no longer green, but pure white. The ribbon around

Toto's neck had also lost its green color and was as white as Dorothy's dress.

The Emerald City was soon left far behind. As they advanced the ground became rougher and hillier, for there were no farms nor houses in this country of the West, and the ground was untilled.

In the afternoon the sun shone hot in their faces, for there were no trees to offer them shade; so that before night Dorothy and Toto and the Lion were tired, and lay down upon the grass and fell asleep, with the Woodman and the Scarecrow keeping watch.

Now the Wicked Witch of the West had but one eye, yet that was as powerful as a telescope, and could see everywhere. So, as she sat in the door of her castle, she happened to look around and saw Dorothy lying asleep, with her friends all about her. They were a long distance off, but the Wicked Witch was angry to find them in her country; so she blew upon a silver whistle that hung around her neck.

At once there came running to her from all directions a pack of great wolves. They had long legs and fierce eyes and sharp teeth.

"Go to those people," said the Witch, "and tear them to pieces."

"Are you not going to make them your slaves?" asked the leader of the wolves.

"No," she answered, "one is of tin, and one of straw; one is a girl and another a Lion. None of them is fit to work, so you may tear them into small pieces."

"Very well," said the wolf, and he dashed away at full speed, followed by the others.

It was lucky the Scarecrow and the Woodman were wide awake and heard the wolves coming.

"This is my fight," said the Woodman; "so get behind me and I will meet them as they come."

He seized his axe, which he had made very sharp, and as the leader of the wolves came on the Tin Woodman swung his arm and chopped the wolf's head from its body, so that it immediately died. As soon as he could raise his axe another wolf came up, and he also fell under the sharp edge of the Tin Woodman's weapon.

There were forty wolves, and forty times a wolf was killed; so that at last they all lay dead in a heap before the Woodman.

Then he put down his axe and sat beside the Scarecrow, who said,

"It was a good fight, friend."

They waited until Dorothy awoke the next morning. The little girl was quite frightened when she saw the great pile of shaggy wolves, but the Tin Woodman told her all. She thanked him for saving them and sat down to breakfast, after which they started again upon their journey.

Now this same morning the Wicked Witch came to the door of her castle and looked out with her one eye that could see far off. She saw all her wolves lying dead, and the strangers still travelling through her country. This made her angrier than before, and she blew her silver whistle twice.

Straightway a great flock of wild crows came flying toward her, enough to darken the sky. And the Wicked Witch said to the King Crow,

"Fly at once to the strangers; peck out their eyes and tear them to pieces."

The wild crows flew in one great flock toward Dorothy and her companions. When the little girl saw them coming she was afraid. But the Scarecrow said,

"This is my battle; so lie down beside me and you will not be harmed."

So they all lay upon the ground except the Scarecrow, and he stood up and stretched out his arms. And when the crows saw him they were frightened, as these birds always are by scarecrows, and did not dare to come any nearer. But the King Crow said,

"It is only a stuffed man. I will peck his eyes out."

The King Crow flew at the Scarecrow, who caught it by the head and twisted its neck until it died. And then another crow flew at him, and the Scarecrow twisted its neck also. There were forty crows, and forty times the Scarecrow twisted a neck, until at last all were lying dead beside him. Then he called to his companions to rise, and again they went upon their journey.

When the Wicked Witch looked out again and saw all her

crows lying in a heap, she got into a terrible rage, and blew three times upon her silver whistle.

Forthwith there was heard a great buzzing in the air, and a swarm of black bees came flying toward her.

"Go to the strangers and sting them to death!" commanded the Witch, and the bees turned and flew rapidly until they came to where Dorothy and her friends were walking. But the Woodman had seen them coming and the Scarecrow had decided what to do.

"Take out my straw and scatter it over the little girl and the dog and the lion," he said to the Woodman, "and the bees cannot sting them." This the Woodman did, and as Dorothy lay close beside the Lion and held Toto in her arms, the straw covered them entirely.

The bees came and found no one but the Woodman to sting, so they flew at him and broke off all their stings against the tin, without hurting the Woodman at all. And as bees cannot live when their stings are broken that was the end of the black bees, and they lay scattered thick about the Woodman, like little heaps of fine coal.

Then Dorothy and the Lion got up, and the girl helped the Tin Woodman put the straw back into the Scarecrow again, until he was as good as ever. So they started upon their journey once more.

The Wicked Witch was so angry when she saw her black bees in little heaps like fine coal that she stamped her foot and tore her hair and gnashed her teeth. And then she called a dozen of her slaves, who were the Winkies, and gave them sharp spears, telling them to go to the strangers and destroy them.

The Winkies were not a brave people, but they had to do as they were told; so they marched away until they came near to Dorothy. Then the Lion gave a great roar and sprang toward them, and the poor Winkies were so frightened that they ran back as fast as they could.

When they returned to the castle the Wicked Witch beat them well with a strap, and sent them back to their work, after which she sat down to think what she should do next. She could not understand how all her plans to destroy these strangers had failed;

but she was a powerful Witch, as well as a wicked one, and she soon made up her mind how to act.

There was, in her cupboard, a Golden Cap, with a circle of diamonds and rubies running round it. This Golden Cap had a charm. Whoever owned it could call three times upon the Winged Monkeys, who would obey any order they were given. But no person could command these strange creatures more than three times. Twice already the Wicked Witch had used the charm of the Cap. Once was when she had made the Winkies her slaves, and set herself to rule over their country. The Winged Monkeys had helped her to do this. The second time was when she had fought against the Great Oz himself, and driven him out of the land of the West. The Winged Monkeys had also helped her in doing this. Only once more could she use this Golden Cap, for which reason she did not like to do so until all her other powers were exhausted. But now that her fierce wolves and her wild crows and her stinging bees were gone, and her slaves had been scared away by the Cowardly Lion, she saw there was only one way left to destroy Dorothy and her friends.

So the Wicked Witch took the Golden Cap from her cupboard and placed it upon her head. Then she stood upon her left foot and said, slowly,

"Ep-pe, pep-pe, kak-ke!"[15]

Next she stood upon her right foot and said,

"Hil-lo, hol-lo, hel-lo!"

After this she stood upon both feet and cried in a loud voice,

"Ziz-zy, zuz-zy, zik!"

Now the charm began to work. The sky was darkened, and a low rumbling sound was heard in the air. There was a rushing of many wings; a great chattering and laughing; and the sun came out of the dark sky to show the Wicked Witch surrounded by a crowd of monkeys, each with a pair of immense and powerful wings on his shoulders.

One, much bigger than the others, seemed to be their leader. He flew close to the Witch and said,

"You have called us for the third and last time. What do you command?"

"Go to the strangers who are within my land and destroy them all except the Lion," said the Wicked Witch. "Bring that beast to me, for I have a mind to harness him like a horse, and make him work."

"Your commands shall be obeyed," said the leader; and then, with a great deal of chattering and noise, the Winged Monkeys flew away to the place where Dorothy and her friends were walking.

Some of the Monkeys seized the Tin Woodman and carried him through the air until they were over a country thickly covered with sharp rocks. Here they dropped the poor Woodman, who fell a great distance to the rocks, where he lay so battered and dented that he could neither move nor groan.

Others of the Monkeys caught the Scarecrow, and with their long fingers pulled all of the straw out of his clothes and head. They made his hat and boots and clothes into a small bundle and threw it into the top branches of a tall tree.

The remaining Monkeys threw pieces of stout rope around the Lion and wound many coils about his body and head and legs, until he was unable to bite or scratch or struggle in any way. Then they lifted him up and flew away with him to the Witch's castle, where he was placed in a small yard with a high iron fence around it, so that he could not escape.

But Dorothy they did not harm at all. She stood, with Toto in her arms, watching the sad fate of her comrades and thinking it would soon be her turn. The leader of the Winged Monkeys flew up to her, his long, hairy arms stretched out and his ugly face grinning terribly, but he saw the mark of the Good Witch's kiss upon her forehead and stopped short, motioning the others not to touch her.

"We dare not harm this little girl," he said to them, "for she is protected by the Power of Good, and that is greater than the Power of Evil. All we can do is to carry her to the castle of the Wicked Witch and leave her there."

So, carefully and gently, they lifted Dorothy in their arms and carried her swiftly through the air until they came to the castle, where they set her down upon the front door step. Then the leader said to the Witch,

## The Search for the Wicked Witch

"We have obeyed you as far as we were able. The Tin Woodman and the Scarecrow are destroyed, and the Lion is tied up in your yard. The little girl we dare not harm, nor the dog she carries in her arms. Your power over our band is now ended, and you will never see us again."

Then all the Winged Monkeys, with much laughing and chattering and noise, flew into the air and were soon out of sight.

The Wicked Witch was both surprised and worried when she saw the mark on Dorothy's forehead, for she knew well that neither the Winged Monkeys nor she, herself, dare hurt the girl in any way. She looked down at Dorothy's feet, and seeing the silver shoes, began to tremble with fear, for she knew what a powerful charm belonged to them. At first the Witch was tempted to run away from Dorothy; but she happened to look into the the child's eyes and saw how simple the soul behind them was, and that the little girl did not know of the wonderful power the silver shoes gave her. So the Wicked Witch laughed to herself, and thought, "I can still make her my slave, for she does not know how to use her power." Then she said to Dorothy, harshly and severely,

"Come with me; and see that you mind everything I tell you, for if you do not I will make an end of you, as I did of the Tin Woodman and the Scarecrow."

Dorothy followed her through many of the beautiful rooms in her castle until they came to the kitchen, where the Witch bade her clean the pots and kettles and sweep the floor and keep the fire fed with wood.

Dorothy went to  work meekly, with her mind made up to work as hard as she could; for she was glad the Wicked Witch had decided not to kill her.

With Dorothy hard at work the Witch thought she would go into the court-yard and harness the Cowardly Lion like a horse; it would amuse her, she was sure, to make him draw her chariot whenever she wished to go to drive. But as she opened the gate the Lion gave a loud roar and bounded at her so fiercely that the Witch was afraid, and ran out and shut the gate again.

"If I cannot harness you," said the Witch to the Lion, speaking through the bars of the gate, "I can starve you. You shall have nothing to eat until you do as I wish."

So after that she took no food to the imprisoned Lion; but every day she came to the gate at noon and asked,

"Are you ready to be harnessed like a horse?"

And the Lion would answer,

"No. If you come in this yard I will bite you."

The reason the Lion did not have to do as the Witch wished was that every night, while the woman was asleep Dorothy carried him food from the cupboard. After he had eaten he would lie down on his bed of straw, and Dorothy would lie beside him and put her head on his soft, shaggy mane, while they talked of their troubles and tried to plan some way to escape. But they could find no way to get out of the castle, for it was constantly guarded by the yellow Winkies, who were slaves of the Wicked Witch and too afraid of her not to do as she told them.

The girl had to work hard during the day, and often the Witch threatened to beat her with the same old umbrella she always carried in her hand. But, in truth, she did not dare to strike Dorothy, because of the mark upon her forehead. The child did not know this, and was full of fear for herself and Toto. Once the Witch struck Toto a blow with her umbrella and the brave little dog flew at her and bit her leg, in return. The Witch did not bleed where she was bitten, for she was so wicked that the blood in her had dried up many years before.

Dorothy's life became very sad as she grew to understand that it would be harder than ever to get back to Kansas and Aunt Em again. Sometimes she would cry bitterly for hours, with Toto sitting at her feet and looking into her face, whining dismally to show how sorry he was for his little mistress. Toto did not really care whether he was in Kansas or the Land of Oz so long as Dorothy was with him; but he knew the little girl was unhappy, and that made him unhappy too.

Now the Wicked Witch had a great longing to have for her own the silver shoes which the girl always wore. Her Bees and her Crows and her Wolves were lying in heaps and drying up, and she had used up all the power of the Golden Cap; but if she could only get hold of the silver shoes they would give her more power than all the other things she had lost. She watched Dorothy carefully, to see if she ever took off her shoes, thinking she might steal them. But the child was so proud of her pretty shoes that she never took them off except at night and when she took her bath. The Witch was too much afraid of the dark to dare go in Dorothy's room at night to take the shoes, and her dread of water was greater than her fear of the dark, so she never came near when Dorothy was bathing. Indeed, the old Witch never touched water, nor ever let water touch her in any way.

But the wicked creature was very cunning, and she finally thought of a trick that would give her what she wanted. She placed a bar of iron in the middle of the kitchen floor, and then by her magic arts made the iron invisible to human eyes. So that when Dorothy walked across the floor she stumbled over the bar, not being able to see it, and fell at full length. She was not much hurt, but in her fall one of the silver shoes came off, and before she could reach it the Witch had snatched it away and put it on her own skinny foot.

The wicked woman was greatly pleased with the success of her trick, for as long as she had one of the shoes she owned half the power of their charm, and Dorothy could not use it against her, even had she known how to do so.

The little girl, seeing she had lost one of her pretty shoes, grew angry, and said to the Witch,

"Give me back my shoe!"

"I will not," retorted the Witch, "for it is now my shoe, and not yours."

"You are a wicked creature!" cried Dorothy. "You have no right to take my shoe from me."

"I shall keep it, just the same," said the Witch, laughing at her, "and some day I shall get the other one from you, too."

This made Dorothy so very angry that she picked up the bucket of water that stood near and dashed it over the Witch, wetting her from head to foot.

Instantly the wicked woman gave a loud cry of fear; and then, as

Dorothy looked at her in wonder, the Witch began to shrink and fall away.

"See what you have done!" she screamed. "In a minute I shall melt away."

"I'm very sorry, indeed," said Dorothy, who was truly frightened to see the Witch actually melting away like brown sugar before her very eyes.

"Didn't you know water would be the end of me?" asked the Witch in a wailing, despairing voice.

"Of course not," answered Dorothy; "how should I?"

"Well, in a few minutes I shall be all melted, and you will have the castle to yourself. I have been wicked in my day, but I never thought a little girl like you would ever be able to melt me and end my wicked deeds. Look out—here I go!"

With these words the Witch fell down in a brown, melted, shapeless mass and began to spread over the clean boards of the kitchen floor. Seeing that she had really melted away to nothing, Dorothy drew another bucket of water and threw it over the mess. She then swept it all out the door. After picking out the silver shoe, which was all that was left of the old woman, she cleaned and dried it with a cloth, and put it on her foot again. Then, being at last free to do as she chose, she ran out to the court-yard to tell the Lion that the Wicked Witch of the West had come to an end, and that they were no longer prisoners in a strange land.

*"The Tinsmiths worked for three days and four nights."*

# The Rescue

THE Cowardly Lion was much pleased to hear that the Wicked Witch had been melted by a bucket of water, and Dorothy at once unlocked the gate of his prison and set him free. They went in together to the castle, where Dorothy's first act was to call all the Winkies together and tell them that they were no longer slaves.

There was great rejoicing among the yellow Winkies, for they had been made to work hard during many years for the Wicked Witch, who had always treated them with great cruelty. They kept this day as a holiday, then and ever after, and spent the time in feasting and dancing.

"If our friends, the Scarecrow and the Tin Woodman, were only with us," said the Lion, "I should be quite happy."

"Don't you suppose we could rescue them?" asked the girl, anxiously.

"We can try," answered the Lion.

So they called the yellow Winkies and asked them if they would help to rescue their friends, and the Winkies said that they would be delighted to do all in their power for Dorothy, who had set them free from bondage. So she chose a number of the Winkies who looked as if they knew the most, and they all started away. They travelled that day and part of the next until they came to the rocky plain where the Tin Woodman lay, all battered and bent. His axe was near him, but the blade was rusted and the handle broken off short.

The Winkies lifted him tenderly in their arms, and carried him back to the yellow castle again, Dorothy shedding a few tears by the way at the sad plight of her old friend, and the Lion looking sober and sorry. When they reached the castle Dorothy said to the Winkies,

"Are any of your people tinsmiths?"

"Oh, yes; some of us are very good tinsmiths," they told her.

"Then bring them to me," she said. And when the tinsmiths came, bringing with them all their tools in baskets, she enquired.

"Can you straighten out those dents in the Tin Woodman, and bend him back into shape again, and solder him together where he is broken?"

The tinsmiths looked the Woodman over carefully and then answered that they thought they could mend him so he would be as good as ever. So they set to work in one of the big yellow rooms of the castle and worked for three days and four nights, hammering and twisting and bending and soldering and polishing and pounding at the legs and body and head of the Tin Woodman, until at last he was straightened out into his old form, and his joints worked as well as ever. To be sure, there were several patches on him, but the tinsmiths did a good job, and as the Woodman was not a vain man he did not mind the patches at all.

When, at last, he walked into Dorothy's room and thanked her for rescuing him, he was so pleased that he wept tears of joy, and Dorothy had to wipe every tear carefully from his face with her apron, so his joints would not be rusted. At the same time her own tears fell thick and fast at the joy of meeting her old friend again, and these tears did not need to be wiped away. As for the Lion, he wiped his eyes so often with the tip of his tail that it became quite wet, and he was obliged to go out into the court-yard and hold it in the sun till it dried.

"If we only had the Scarecrow with us again," said the Tin Woodman, when Dorothy had finished telling him everything that had happened, "I should be quite happy."

"We must try to find him," said the girl.

So she called the Winkies to help her, and they walked all that day and part of the next until they came to the tall tree in the branches of which the Winged Monkeys had tossed the Scarecrow's clothes.

It was a very tall tree, and the trunk was so smooth that no one could climb it; but the Woodman said at once,

"I'll chop it down, and then we can get the Scarecrow's clothes."

# The Rescue

Now while the tinsmiths had been at work mending the Woodman himself, another of the Winkies, who was a goldsmith, had made an axe-handle of solid gold and fitted it to the Woodman's axe, instead of the old broken handle. Others polished the blade until all the rust was removed and it glistened like burnished silver.

As soon as he had spoken, the Tin Woodman began to chop, and in a short time the tree fell over with a crash, when the Scarecrow's clothes fell out of the branches and rolled off on the ground.

Dorothy picked them up and had the Winkies carry them back to the castle, where they were stuffed with nice, clean straw; and, behold! here was the Scarecrow, as good as ever, thanking them over and over again for saving him.

Now they were reunited, Dorothy and her friends spent a few happy days at the yellow castle, where they found everything they needed to make them comfortable. But one day the girl thought of Aunt Em, and said,

"We must go back to Oz, and claim his promise."

"Yes," said the Woodman, "at last I shall get my heart."

"And I shall get my brains," added the Scarecrow, joyfully.

"And I shall get my courage," said the Lion, thoughtfully.

"And I shall get back to Kansas," cried Dorothy, clapping her hands. "Oh, let us start for the Emerald City to-morrow!"

This they decided to do. The next day they called the Winkies together and bade them good-bye. The Winkies were sorry to have them go, and they had grown so found of the Tin Woodman that they begged him to stay and rule over them and the Yellow Land of the West. Finding they were determined to go, the Winkies gave Toto and the Lion each a golden collar; and to Dorothy they presented a beautiful bracelet, studded with diamonds; and to the Scarecrow they gave a gold-headed walking stick, to keep him from stumbling; and to the Tin Woodman they offered a silver oil-can, inlaid with gold and set with precious jewels.

Every one of the travellers made the Winkies a pretty speech in return, and all shook hands with them until their arms ached.

Dorothy went to the Witch's cupboard to fill her basket with food for the journey, and there she saw the Golden Cap. She tried it on her own head and found that it fitted her exactly. She did not know anything about the charm of the Golden Cap, but she saw that it was pretty, so she made up her mind to wear it and carry her sunbonnet in the basket.

Then, being prepared for the journey, they all started for the Emerald City; and the Winkies gave them three cheers and many good wishes to carry with them.

# The Winged Monkeys

YOU will remember there was no road—not even a pathway—between the castle of the Wicked Witch and the Emerald City. When the four travellers went in search of the Witch she had seen them coming, and so sent the Winged Monkeys to bring them to her. It was much harder to find their way back through the big fields of buttercups and bright daisies than it was being carried. They knew, of course, they must go straight east, toward the rising sun; and they started off in the right way. But at noon, when the sun was over their heads, they did not know which was east and which was west, and that was the reason they were lost in the great fields. They kept on walking, however, and at night the moon came out and shone brightly. So they lay down among the sweet smelling scarlet flowers and slept soundly until morning—all but the Scarecrow and the Tin Woodman.

The next morning the sun was behind a cloud, but they started on, as if they were quite sure which way they were going.

"If we walk far enough," said Dorothy, "we shall sometime come to some place, I am sure."

But day by day passed away, and they still saw nothing before them but the scarlet fields. The Scarecrow began to grumble a bit.

"We have surely lost our way," he said, "and unless we find it again in time to reach the Emerald City I shall never get my brains."

"Nor I my heart," declared the Tin Woodman. "It seems to me I can scarcely wait till I get to Oz, and you must admit this is a very long journey."

"You see," said the Cowardly Lion, with a whimper, "I haven't the courage to keep tramping forever, without getting anywhere at all."

Then Dorothy lost heart. She sat down on the grass and looked at her companions, and they sat down and looked at her, and Toto found that for the first time in his life he was too tired to chase a butterfly that flew past his head; so he put out his tongue and panted and looked at Dorothy as if to ask what they should do next.

"Suppose we call the Field-Mice," she suggested. "They could probably tell us the way to the Emerald City."

"To be sure they could," cried the Scarecrow; "why didn't we think of that before?"

Dorothy blew the little whistle she had always carried about her neck since the Queen of the Mice had given it to her. In a few minutes they heard the pattering of tiny feet, and many of the small gray mice came running up to her. Among them was the Queen herself, who asked, in her squeaky little voice,

"What can I do for my friends?"

"We have lost our way," said Dorothy. "Can you tell us where the Emerald City is?"

"Certainly," answered the Queen; "but it is a great way off, for you have had it at your backs all this time." Then she noticed Dorothy's Golden Cap, and said, "Why don't you use the charm of the Cap, and call the Winged Monkeys to you? They will carry you to the City of Oz in less than an hour."

"I didn't know there was a charm," answered Dorothy, in surprise. "What is it?"

"It is written inside the Golden Cap," replied the Queen of the Mice; "but if you are going to call the Winged Monkeys we must run away, for they are full of mischief and think it great fun to plague us."

"Won't they hurt me?" asked the girl, anxiously.

"Oh, no; they must obey the wearer of the Cap. Good-bye!" And she scampered out of sight, with all the mice hurrying after her.[16]

Dorothy looked inside the Golden Cap and saw some words written upon the lining. These, she thought, must be the charm, so she read the directions carefully and put the Cap upon her head.

"Ep-pe, pep-pe, kak-ke!" she said, standing on her left foot.

# The Winged Monkeys

"What did you say?" asked the Scarecrow, who did not know what she was doing.

"Hil-lo, hol-lo, hel-lo!" Dorothy went on, standing this time on her right foot.

"Hello!" replied the Tin Woodman, calmly.

"Ziz-zy, zuz-zy, zik!" said Dorothy, who was now standing on both feet. This ended the saying of the charm, and they heard a great chattering and flapping of wings, as the band of Winged Monkeys flew up to them. The King bowed low before Dorothy, and asked,

"What is your command?"

"We wish to go to the Emerald City," said the child, "and we have lost our way."

"We will carry you," replied the King, and no sooner had he spoken than two of the Monkeys caught Dorothy in their arms and flew away with her. Others took the Scarecrow and the Woodman and the Lion, and one little Monkey seized Toto and flew after them, although the dog tried hard to bite him.

The Scarecrow and the Tin Woodman were rather frightened at first, for they remembered how badly the Winged Monkeys had treated them before; but they saw that no harm was intended, so they rode through the air quite cheerfully, and had a fine time looking at the pretty gardens and woods far below them.

Dorothy found herself riding easily between two of the biggest Monkeys, one of them the King himself. They had made a chair of their hands and were careful not to hurt her.

"Why do you have to obey the charm of the Golden Cap?" she asked.

"That is a long story," answered the King, with a laugh; "but as we have a long journey before us I will pass the time by telling you about it, if you wish."

"I shall be glad to hear it," she replied.

"Once," began the leader, "we were a free people, living happily in the great forest, flying from tree to tree, eating nuts and fruit, and doing just as we pleased without calling anybody master. Perhaps some of us were rather too full of mischief at times, flying down to pull the tails of the animals that had no wings, chasing birds, and throwing nuts at the people who walked in the forest.

But we were careless and happy and full of fun, and enjoyed every minute of the day. This was many years ago, long before Oz came out of the clouds to rule over this land.

"There lived here then, away at the North, a beautiful princess, who was also a powerful sorceress. All her magic was used to help the people, and she was never known to hurt anyone who was good. Her name was Gayelette,[17] and she lived in a handsome palace built from great blocks of ruby. Everyone loved her, but her greatest sorrow was that she could find no one to love in return, since all the men were much too stupid and ugly to mate with one so beautiful and wise. At last, however, she found a boy who was handsome and manly and wise beyond his years. Gayelette made up her mind that when he grew to be a man she would make him her husband, so she took him to her ruby palace and used all her magic powers to make him as strong and good and lovely as any woman could wish. When he grew to manhood, Quelala, as he was called, was said to be the best and wisest man in all the land, while his manly beauty was so great that Gayelette loved him dearly, and hastened to make everything ready for the wedding.

"My grandfather was at that time the King of the Winged Monkeys which lived in the forest near Gayelette's palace, and the old fellow loved a joke better than a good dinner. One day, just before the wedding, my grandfather was flying out with his band when he saw Quelala walking beside the river. He was dressed in a rich costume of pink silk and purple velvet, and my grandfather thought he would see what he could do. At his word the band flew down and seized Quelala, carried him in their arms until they were over the middle of the river, and then dropped him into the water.

" 'Swim out, my fine fellow,' cried my grandfather, 'and see if the water has spotted your clothes.' Quelala was much too wise not to swim, and he was not in the least spoiled by all his good fortune. He laughed, when he came to the top of the water, and swam in to shore. But when Gayelette came running out to him she found his silks and velvet all ruined by the river.

"The princess was very angry, and she knew, of course, who did it. She had all the Winged Monkeys brought before her, and she said at first that their wings should be tied and they should be treated as they had treated Quelala, and dropped in the river. But my grandfather pleaded hard, for he knew the Monkeys would drown in the river with their wings tied, and Quelala said a kind word for them also; so that Gayelette finally spared them, on condition that the Winged Monkeys should ever after do three times the bidding of the owner of the Golden Cap. This Cap had been made for a wedding present to Quelala, and it is said to have cost the princess half her kingdom. Of course my grandfather and all the other Monkeys at once agreed to the condition, and that is how it happens that we are three times the slaves of the owner of the Golden Cap, whomsoever he may be."

"And what became of them?" asked Dorothy, who had been greatly interested in the story.

"Quelala being the first owner of the Golden Cap," replied the Monkey, "he was the first to lay his wishes upon us. As his bride could not bear the sight of us, he called us all to him in the forest after he had married her and ordered us to always keep where she could never again set eyes on a Winged Monkey, which we were glad to do, for were were all afraid of her.

"This was all we ever had to do until the Golden Cap fell into the hands of the Wicked Witch of the West, who made us enslave the Winkies, and afterward drive Oz himself out of the Land of the West. Now the Golden Cap is yours, and three times you have the right to lay your wishes upon us."

As the Monkey King finished his story Dorothy looked down and saw the green, shining walls of the Emerald City before them. She wondered at the rapid flight of the Monkeys, but was glad the journey was over. The strange creatures set the travellers down carefully before the gate of the City, the King bowed low to Dorothy, and then flew swiftly away, followed by all his band.

"That was a good ride," said the little girl.

"Yes, and a quick way out of our troubles," replied the Lion. "How lucky it was you brought away that wonderful Cap!"

*"Exactly so! I am a humbug."*

# The Discovery of Oz,
# the Terrible

THE four travellers walked up to the great gate of the Emerald
City and rang the bell. After ringing several times it was
opened by the same Guardian of the Gates they had met before.

"What! are you back again?" he asked, in surprise.

"Do you not see us?" answered the Scarecrow.

"But I thought you had gone to visit the Wicked Witch of the
West."

"We did visit her," said the Scarecrow.

"And she let you go again?" asked the man, in wonder.

"She could not help it, for she is melted," explained the Scarecrow.

"Melted! Well, that is good news, indeed," said the man. "Who
melted her?"

"It was Dorothy," said the Lion, gravely.

"Good gracious!" exclaimed the man, and he bowed very low
indeed before her.

Then he led them into his little room and locked the spectacles
from the great box on all their eyes, just as he had done before.
Afterward they passed on through the gate into the Emerald City,
and when the people heard from the Guardian of the Gates that
they had melted the Wicked Witch of the West they all gathered
around the travellers and followed them in a great crowd to the
Palace of Oz.

The soldier with the green whiskers was still on guard before
the door, but he let them in at once and they were again met by
the beautiful green girl, who showed each of them to their old

rooms at once, so they might rest until the Great Oz was ready to receive them.

The soldier had the news carried straight to Oz that Dorothy and the other travellers had come back again, after destroying the Wicked Witch; but Oz made no reply. They thought the Great Wizard would send for them at once, but he did not. They had no word from him the next day, nor the next, nor the next. The waiting was tiresome and wearing, and at last they grew vexed that Oz should treat them in so poor a fashion, after sending them to undergo hardships and slavery. So the Scarecrow at last asked the green girl to take another message to Oz, saying if he did not let them in to see him at once they would call the Winged Monkeys to help them, and find out whether he kept his promises or not. When the Wizard was given this message he was so frightened that he sent word for them to come to the Throne Room at four minutes after nine o'clock the next morning. He had once met the Winged Monkeys in the Land of the West, and he did not wish to meet them again.

The four travellers passed a sleepless night, each thinking of the gift Oz had promised to bestow upon him. Dorothy fell asleep only once, and then she dreamed she was in Kansas, where Aunt Em was telling her how glad she was to have her little girl at home again.

Promptly at nine o'clock the next morning the green whiskered soldier came to them, and four minutes later they all went into the Throne Room of the Great Oz.

Of course each one of them expected to see the Wizard in the shape he had taken before, and all were greatly surprised when they looked about and saw no one at all in the room. They kept close to the door and closer to one another, for the stillness of the empty room was more dreadful than any of the forms they had seen Oz take.

Presently they heard a Voice, seeming to come from somewhere near the top of the great dome, and it said, solemnly.

"I am Oz, the Great and Terrible. Why do you seek me?"

They looked again in every part of the room, and then, seeing no one, Dorothy asked,

# The Discovery of Oz, the Terrible

"Where are you?"

"I am everywhere," answered the Voice, "but to the eyes of common mortals I am invisible. I will now seat myself upon my throne, that you may converse with me." Indeed, the Voice seemed just then to come straight from the throne itself; so they walked toward it and stood in a row while Dorothy said:

"We have come to claim our promise, O Oz."

"What promise?" asked Oz.

"You promised to send me back to Kansas when the Wicked Witch was destroyed," said the girl.

"And you promised to give me brains," said the Scarecrow.

"And you promised to give me a heart," said the Tin Woodman.

"And you promised to give me courage," said the Cowardly Lion.

"Is the Wicked Witch really destroyed?" asked the Voice, and Dorothy thought it trembled a little.

"Yes," she answered, "I melted her with a bucket of water."

"Dear me," said the Voice; "how sudden! Well, come to me tomorrow, for I must have time to think it over."

"You've had plenty of time already," said the Tin Woodman, angrily.

"We shan't wait a day longer," said the Scarecrow.

"You must keep your promises to us!" exclaimed Dorothy.

The Lion thought it might be as well to frighten the Wizard, so he gave a large, loud roar, which was so fierce and dreadful that Toto jumped away from him in alarm and tipped over the screen that stood in a corner. As it fell with a crash they looked that way, and the next moment all of them were filled with wonder. For they saw standing in just the spot the screen had hidden, a little, old man, with a bald head and a wrinkled face, who seemed to be as much surprised as they were. The Tin Woodman, raising his axe, rushed toward the little man and cried out,

"Who are you?"

"I am Oz, the Great and Terrible," said the little man, in a trembling voice, "but don't strike me—please don't!—and I'll do anything you want me to."

Our friends looked at him in surprise and dismay.

"I thought Oz was a great Head," said Dorothy.

"And I thought Oz was a lovely Lady," said the Scarecrow.

"And I thought Oz was a terrible Beast," said the Tin Woodman.

"And I thought Oz was a Ball of Fire!" exclaimed the Lion.

"No; you are all wrong," said the little man, meekly. "I have been making believe."

"Making believe!" cried Dorothy. "Are you not a Great Wizard?"

"Hush, my dear," he said; "don't speak so loud, or you will be overheard—and I should be ruined. I'm supposed to be a Great Wizard."

"And aren't you?" she asked.

"Not a bit of it, my dear; I'm just a common man."

"You're more than that," said the Scarecrow, in a grieved tone; "you're a humbug."

"Exactly so!" declared the little man, rubbing his hands together as if it pleased him; "I am a humbug."

"But this is terrible," said the Tin Woodman; "how shall I ever get my heart?"

"Or I my courage?" asked the Lion.

"Or I my brains?" wailed the Scarecrow, wiping the tears from his eyes with his coat-sleeve.

"My dear friends," said Oz, "I pray you not to speak of these little things. Think of me, and the terrible trouble I'm in at being found out."

"Doesn't anyone else know you're a humbug?" asked Dorothy.

"No one knows it but you four—and myself," replied Oz. "I have fooled everyone so long that I thought I should never be found out. It was a great mistake my ever letting you into the Throne Room. Usually I will not see even my subjects, and so they believe I am something terrible."

"But, I don't understand," said Dorothy, in bewilderment. "How was it that you appeared to me as a great Head?"

"That was one of my tricks," answered Oz. "Step this way, please, and I will tell you all about it."

He led the way to a small chamber in the rear of the Throne Room, and they all followed him. He pointed to one corner, in which lay the Great Head, made out of many thicknesses of paper, and with a carefully painted face.

"This I hung from the ceiling by a wire," said Oz; "I stood behind the screen and pulled a thread, to make the eyes move and the mouth open."

"But how about the voice?" she enquired.

"Oh, I am a ventriloquist," said the little man, "and I can throw the sound of my voice wherever I wish; so that you thought it was coming out of the Head. Here are the other things I used to deceive you." He showed the Scarecrow the dress and the mask he had worn when he seemed to be the lovely Lady; and the Tin Woodman saw that his terrible Beast was nothing but a lot of skins, sewn together, with slats to keep their sides out. As for the Ball of Fire, the false Wizard had hung that also from the ceiling. It was really a ball of cotton, but when oil was poured upon it the ball burned fiercely.

"Really," said the Scarecrow, "you ought to be ashamed of yourself for being such a humbug."

"I am—I certainly am," answered the little man, sorrowfully; "but it was the only thing I could do. Sit down, please, there are plenty of chairs; and I will tell you my story."

So they sat down and listened while he told the following tale: "I was born in Omaha—"[18]

"Why, that isn't very far from Kansas!" cried Dorothy.

"No; but it's farther from here," he said, shaking his head at her, sadly. "When I grew up I became a ventriloquist, and at that I was very well trained by a great master. I can imitate any kind of a bird or beast." Here he mewed so like a kitten that Toto pricked up his ears and looked everywhere to see where she was. "After a time," continued Oz, "I tired of that, and became a balloonist."

"What is that?" asked Dorothy.

"A man who goes up in a balloon on circus day, so as to draw a crowd of people together and get them to pay to see the circus," he explained.

"Oh," she said; "I know."

"Well, one day I went up in a balloon and the ropes got twisted, so that I couldn't come down again. It went way up above the clouds, so far that a current of air struck it and carried it many, many miles away. For a day and a night I travelled through the air, and on the morning of the second day I awoke and found the balloon floating over a strange and beautiful country.

"It came down gradually, and I was not hurt a bit. But I found myself in the midst of a strange people, who, seeing me come from the clouds, thought I was a Great Wizard. Of course I let them think so, because they were afraid of me, and promised to do anything I wished them to.

"Just to amuse myself, and keep the good people busy, I ordered them to build this City, and my palace; and they did it all willingly and well. Then I thought, as the country was so green and beautiful, I would call it the Emerald City, and to make the name fit better I put green spectacles on all the people, so that everything they saw was green."

"But isn't everything here green?" asked Dorothy.

"No more than in any other city," replied Oz; "but when you wear green spectacles, why of course everything you see looks green to you.[19] The Emerald City was built a great many years ago, for I was a young man when the balloon brought me here, and I am a very old man now.[20] But my people have worn green glasses on their eyes so long that most of them think it really is an Emerald City, and it certainly is a beautiful place, abounding in jewels and precious metals, and every good thing that is needed to make one happy. I have been good to the people, and they like me; but ever since this Palace was built I have shut myself up and would not see any of them.

"One of my greatest fears was the Witches, for while I had no magical powers at all I soon found out that the Witches were really able to do wonderful things. There were four of them in this country, and they ruled the people who live in the North and South and East and West. Fortunately, the Witches of the North and South were good, and I knew they would do me no harm; but the Witches of the East and West were terribly wicked, and had they not thought I was more powerful than they themselves, they would surely have destroyed me. As it was, I lived in deadly fear of them for many years; so you can imagine how pleased I was when I heard your house had fallen on the Wicked Witch of the East. When you came to me I was willing to promise anything if you would only do away with the other Witch; but, now that you have melted her, I am ashamed to say that I cannot keep my promises."

"I think you are a very bad man," said Dorothy.

"Oh, no, my dear; I'm really a very good man; but I'm a very bad Wizard, I must admit."

"Can't you give me brains?" asked the Scarecrow.

"You don't need them. You are learning something every day. A baby has brains, but it doesn't know much. Experience is the only thing that brings knowledge, and the longer you are on earth the more experience you are sure to get."

"That may all be true," said the Scarecrow, "but I shall be very unhappy unless you give me brains."

The false wizard looked at him carefully.

"Well," he said, with a sigh, "I'm not much of a magician, as I said; but if you will come to me to-morrow morning, I will stuff your head with brains. I cannot tell you how to use them, however; you must find that out for yourself."

"Oh, thank you—thank you!" cried the Scarecrow. "I'll find a way to use them, never fear!"

"But how about my courage?" asked the Lion, anxiously.

"You have plenty of courage, I am sure," answered Oz. "All you need is confidence in yourself. There is no living thing that is not afraid when it faces danger. True courage is in facing danger when you are afraid, and that kind of courage you have in plenty."

"Perhaps I have, but I'm scared just the same," said the Lion. "I shall really be very unhappy unless you give me the sort of courage that makes one forget he is afraid."

"Very well; I will give you that sort of courage to-morrow," replied Oz.

"How about my heart?" asked the Tin Woodman.

"Why, as for that," answered Oz, "I think you are wrong to want a heart. It makes most people unhappy. If you only knew it, you are in luck not to have a heart."

"That must be a matter of opinion," said the Tin Woodman.

"For my part, I will bear all the unhappiness without a murmur, if you will give me the heart."

"Very well," answered Oz, meekly. "Come to me to-morrow and you shall have a heart. I have played Wizard for so many years that I may as well continue the part a little longer."

"And now," said Dorothy, "how am I to get back to Kansas?"

"We shall have to think about that," replied the little man. "Give me two or three days to consider the matter and I'll try to find a way to carry you over the desert. In the meantime you shall all be treated as my guests, and while you live in the Palace my people will wait upon you and obey your slightest wish. There is only one thing I ask in return for my help—such as it is. You must keep my secret and tell no one I am a humbug."

They agreed to say nothing of what they had learned, and went back to their rooms in high spirits. Even Dorothy had hope that "The Great and Terrible Humbug," as she called him, would find a way to send her back to Kansas, and if he did that she was willing to forgive him everything.

" 'I feel wise, indeed,' said the Scarecrow."

# The Magic Art
# of the Great Humbug

NEXT morning the Scarecrow said to his friends:
"Congratulate me. I am going to Oz to get my brains at last. When I return I shall be as other men are."

"I have always liked you as you were," said Dorothy, simply.

"It is kind of you to like a Scarecrow," he replied. "But surely you will think more of me when you hear the splendid thoughts my new brain is going to turn out." Then he said good-bye to them all in a cheerful voice and went to the Throne Room, where he rapped upon the door.

"Come in," said Oz.

The Scarecrow went in and found the little man sitting down by the window, engaged in deep thought.

"I have come for my brains," remarked the Scarecrow, a little uneasily.

"Oh, yes; sit down in that chair, please," replied Oz. "You must excuse me for taking your head off, but I shall have to do it in order to put your brains in their proper place."

"That's all right," said the Scarecrow. "You are quite welcome to take my head off, as long as it will be a better one when you put it on again."

So the Wizard unfastened his head and emptied out the straw. Then he entered the back room and took up a measure of bran, which he mixed with a great many pins and needles. Having shaken them together thoroughly, he filled the top of the Scarecrow's head with the mixture and stuffed the rest of the space with straw, to hold it in place. When he had fastened the Scarecrow's head on his body again he said to him,

"Hereafter you will be a great man, for I have given you a lot of bran-new brains."

The Scarecrow was both pleased and proud at the fulfillment of his greatest wish, and having thanked Oz warmly he went back to his friends.

Dorothy looked at him curiously. His head was quite bulging out at the top with brains.

"How do you feel?" she asked.

"I feel wise, indeed," he answered, earnestly. "When I get used to my brains I shall know everything."

"Why are those needles and pins sticking out of your head?" asked the Tin Woodman.

"That is proof that he is sharp," remarked the Lion.

"Well, I must go to Oz and get my heart," said the Woodman. So he walked to the Throne Room and knocked at the door.

"Come in," called Oz, and the Woodman entered and said,

"I have come for my heart."

"Very well," answered the little man. "But I shall have to cut a hole in your breast, so I can put your heart in the right place. I hope it won't hurt you."

"Oh, no," answered the Woodman. "I shall not feel it at all."

So Oz brought a pair of tinners' shears and cut a small, square hole in the left side of the Tin Woodman's breast. Then, going to a chest of drawers, he took out a pretty heart, made entirely of silk[21] and stuffed with sawdust.

"Isn't it a beauty?" he asked.

"It is, indeed!" replied the Woodman, who was greatly pleased. "But is it a kind heart?"

"Oh, very!" answered Oz. He put the heart in the Woodman's breast and then replaced the square of tin, soldering it neatly together where it had been cut.

"There," said he; "now you have a heart that any man might be proud of. I'm sorry I had to put a patch on your breast, but it really couldn't be helped."

"Never mind the patch!" exclaimed the happy Woodman. "I am very grateful to you, and shall never forget your kindness."

"Don't speak of it," replied Oz.

Then the Tin Woodman went back to his friends, who wished him every joy on account of his good fortune.

The Lion now walked to the Throne Room and knocked at the door.

"Come in," said Oz.

"I have come for my courage," announced the Lion, entering the room.

"Very well," answered the little man; "I will get it for you."

He went to a cupboard and reaching up to a high shelf took down a square green bottle, the contents of which he poured into a green-gold dish, beautifully carved. Placing this before the Cowardly Lion, who sniffed at it as if he did not like it, the Wizard said,

"Drink."

"What is it?" asked the Lion.

"Well," answered Oz, "if it were inside of you, it would be courage. You know, of course, that courage is always inside one; so that this really cannot be called courage until you have swallowed it. Therefore I advise you to drink it as soon as possible."

The Lion hesitated no longer, but drank till the dish was empty.

"How do you feel now?" asked Oz.

"Full of courage," replied the Lion, who went joyfully back to his friends to tell them of his good fortune.

Oz, left to himself, smiled to think of his success in giving the Scarecrow and the Tin Woodman and the Lion exactly what they thought they wanted. "How can I help being a humbug," he said, "when all these people make me do things that everybody knows can't be done? It was easy to make the Scarecrow and the Lion and the Woodman happy, because they imagined I could do anything. But it will take more than imagination to carry Dorothy back to Kansas, and I'm sure I don't know how it can be done."

# How the Balloon
# Was Launched

FOR three days Dorothy heard nothing from Oz. These were sad days for the little girl, although her friends were all quite happy and contented. The Scarecrow told them there were wonderful thoughts in his head; but he would not say what they were because he knew no one could understand them but himself. When the Tin Woodman walked about he felt his heart rattling around in his breast; and he told Dorothy he had discovered it to be a kinder and more tender heart than the one he had owned when he was made of flesh. The Lion declared he was afraid of nothing on earth, and would gladly face an army of men or a dozen of the fierce Kalidahs.

Thus each of the little party was satisfied except Dorothy, who longed more than ever to get back to Kansas.

On the fourth day, to her great joy, Oz sent for her, and when she entered the Throne Room he said, pleasantly:

"Sit down, my dear; I think I have found the way to get you out of this country."

"And back to Kansas?" she asked, eagerly.

"Well, I'm not sure about Kansas," said Oz; "for I haven't the faintest notion which way it lies. But the first thing to do is to cross the desert, and then it should be easy to find your way home."

"How can I cross the desert?" she enquired.

"Well, I'll tell you what I think," said the little man. "You see, when I came to this country it was in a balloon. You also came through the air, being carried by a cyclone. So I believe the best way to get across the desert will be through the air. Now, it is quite beyond my powers to make a cyclone; but I've been thinking the matter over, and I believe I can make a balloon."

"How?" asked Dorothy.

"A balloon," said Oz, "is made of silk, which is coated with glue to keep the gas in it. I have plenty of silk in the Palace, so it will be no trouble for us to make the balloon. But in all this country there is no gas to fill the balloon with, to make it float."

"If it won't float," remarked Dorothy, "it will be of no use to us."

"True," answered Oz. "But there is another way to make it float, which is to fill it with hot air. Hot air isn't as good as gas, for if the air should get cold the balloon would come down in the desert, and we should be lost."

"We!" exclaimed the girl; "are you going with me?"

"Yes, of course," replied Oz. "I am tired of being such a humbug. If I should go out of this Palace my people would soon discover I am not a Wizard, and then they would be vexed with me for having deceived them. So I have to stay shut up in these rooms all day, and it gets tiresome. I'd much rather go back to Kansas with you and be in a circus again."

"I shall be glad to have your company," said Dorothy.

"Thank you," he answered. "Now, if you will help me sew the silk together, we will begin to work on our balloon."

So Dorothy took a needle and thread, and as fast as Oz cut the strips of silk into proper shape the girl sewed them neatly together. First there was a strip of light green silk, then a strip of dark green and then a strip of emerald green; for Oz had a fancy to make the balloon in different shades of the color about them. It took three days to sew all the strips together, but when it was finished they had a big bag of green silk more than twenty feet long.

Then Oz painted it on the inside with a coat of thin glue, to make it air-tight, after which he announced that the balloon was ready.

"But we must have a basket to ride in," he said. So he sent the soldier with the green whiskers for a big clothes basket, which he fastened with many ropes to the bottom of the balloon.

# How the Balloon Was Launched

When it was all ready, Oz sent word to his people that he was going to make a visit to a great brother Wizard who lived in the clouds. The news spread rapidly throughout the city and everyone came to see the wonderful sight.

Oz ordered the balloon carried out in front of the Palace, and the people gazed upon it with much curiosity. The Tin Woodman had chopped a big pile of wood, and now he made a fire of it, and Oz held the bottom of the balloon over the fire so that the hot air that arose from it would be caught in the silken bag. Gradually the balloon swelled out and rose into the air, until finally the basket just touched the ground.

Then Oz got into the basket and said to all the people in a loud voice:

"I am now going away to make a visit. While I am gone the Scarecrow will rule over you. I command you to obey him as you would me."

The balloon was by this time tugging hard at the rope that held it to the ground, for the air within it was hot, and this made it so much lighter in weight than the air without that it pulled hard to rise into the sky.

"Come, Dorothy!" cried the Wizard; "hurry up, or the balloon will fly away."

"I can't find Toto anywhere," replied Dorothy, who did not wish to leave her little dog behind. Toto had run into the crowd to bark at a kitten, and Dorothy at last found him. She picked him up and ran toward the balloon.

She was within a few steps of it, and Oz was holding out his hands to help her into the basket, when, crack! went the ropes, and the balloon rose into the air without her.

"Come back!" she screamed; "I want to go, too!"

"I can't come back, my dear," called Oz from the basket. "Good-bye!"

"Good-bye" shouted everyone, and all eyes were turned upward to where the Wizard was riding in the basket, rising every moment farther and farther into the sky.

And that was the last any of them ever saw of Oz, the Wonderful Wizard, though he may have reached Omaha safely, and be there now, for all we know. But the people remembered him lovingly, and said to one another,

"Oz was always our friend. When he was here he built for us this beautiful Emerald City, and now he is gone he has left the Wise Scarecrow to rule over us."

Still, for many days they grieved over the loss of the Wonderful Wizard, and would not be comforted.

# Away to the South

DOROTHY wept bitterly at the passing of her hope to get home to Kansas again; but when she thought it all over she was glad she had not gone up in a balloon. And she also felt sorry at losing Oz, and so did her companions.

The Tin Woodman came to her and said,

"Truly I should be ungrateful if I failed to mourn for the man who gave me my lovely heart. I should like to cry a little because Oz is gone, if you will kindly wipe away my tears, so that I shall not rust."

"With pleasure," she answered, and brought a towel at once. Then the Tin Woodman wept for several minutes, and she watched the tears carefully and wiped them away with the towel. When he had finished he thanked her kindly and oiled himself thoroughly with his jewelled oil-can, to guard against mishap.

The Scarecrow was now the ruler of the Emerald City, and although he was not a Wizard the people were proud of him. "For," they said, "there is not another city in all the world that is ruled by a stuffed man." And, so far as they knew, they were quite right.[22]

The morning after the balloon had gone up with Oz the four travellers met in the Throne Room and talked matters over. The Scarecrow sat in the big throne and the others stood respectfully before him.

"We are not so unlucky," said the new ruler; "for this Palace and the Emerald City belong to us, and we can do just as we please. When I remember that a short time ago I was up on a pole in a farmer's cornfield, and that I am now the ruler of this beautiful City, I am quite satisfied with my lot."

"I also," said the Tin Woodman, "am well pleased with my new heart; and, really, that was the only thing I wished in all the world."

"For my part, I am content in knowing I am brave as any beast that ever lived, if not braver," said the Lion, modestly,

"If Dorothy would only be contented to live in the Emerald City," continued the Scarecrow, "we might all be happy together."

"But I don't want to live here," cried Dorothy. "I want to go to Kansas, and live with Aunt Em and Uncle Henry."

"Well, then, what can be done?" enquired the Woodman.

The Scarecrow decided to think, and he thought so hard that the pins and needles began to stick out of his brains. Finally he said:

"Why not call the Winged Monkeys, and ask them to carry you over the desert?"

"I never thought of that!" said Dorothy, joyfully. "It's just the thing. I'll go at once for the Golden Cap."

When she brought it into the Throne Room she spoke the magic words, and soon the band of Winged Monkeys flew in through an open window and stood beside her.

"This is the second time you have called us," said the Monkey King, bowing before the little girl. "What do you wish?"

"I want you to fly with me to Kansas," said Dorothy.

But the Monkey King shook his head.

"That cannot be done," he said. "We belong to this country alone, and cannot leave it. There has never been a Winged Monkey in Kansas yet, and I suppose there never will be, for they don't belong there. We shall be glad to serve you in any way in our power, but we cannot cross the desert. Good-bye."

And with another bow the Monkey King spread his wings and flew away through the window, followed by all his band.

Dorothy was almost ready to cry with disappointment.

"I have wasted the charm of the Golden Cap to no purpose," she said, "for the Winged Monkeys cannot help me."

"It is certainly too bad!" said the tender hearted Woodman.

The Scarecrow was thinking again, and his head bulged out so horribly that Dorothy feared it would burst.

"Let us call in the soldier with the green whiskers," he said, "and ask his advice."

So the soldier was summoned and entered the Throne Room

timidly, for while Oz was alive he never was allowed to come further than the door.

"This little girl," said the Scarecrow to the soldier, "wishes to cross the desert. How can she do so?"

"I cannot tell," answered the soldier; "for nobody has ever crossed the desert, unless it is Oz himself."

"Is there no one who can help me?" asked Dorothy, earnestly.

"Glinda might," he suggested.

"Who is Glinda?" enquired the Scarecrow.

"The Witch of the South. She is the most powerful of all the Witches, and rules over the Quadlings. Besides, her castle stands on the edge of the desert, so she may know a way to cross it."

"Glinda is a good Witch, isn't she?" asked the child.

"The Quadlings think she is good," said the soldier, "and she is kind to everyone. I have heard that Glinda is a beautiful woman, who knows how to keep young in spite of the many years she has lived."

"How can I get to her castle?" asked Dorothy.

"The road is straight to the South," he answered, "but it is said to be full of dangers to travellers. There are wild beasts in the woods, and a race of queer men who do not like strangers to cross their country. For this reason none of the Quadlings ever come to the Emerald City."

The soldier then left them and the Scarecrow said,

"It seems, in spite of dangers, that the best thing Dorothy can do is to travel to the Land of the South and ask Glinda to help her. For, of course, if Dorothy stays here she will never get back to Kansas."

"You must have been thinking again," remarked the Tin Woodman.

"I have," said the Scarecrow.

"I shall go with Dorothy," declared the Lion, "for I am tired of your city and long for the woods and the country again. I am really a wild beast, you know. Besides, Dorothy will need someone to protect her."

"That is true," agreed the Woodman. "My axe may be of service to her; so I, also, will go with her to the Land of the South."

"When shall we start?" asked the Scarecrow.

"Are you going?" they asked, in surprise.

"Certainly. If it wasn't for Dorothy I should never have had brains. She lifted me from the pole in the cornfield and brought me to the Emerald City. So my good luck is all due to her, and I shall never leave her until she starts back to Kansas for good and all."

"Thank you," said Dorothy, gratefully. "You are all very kind to me. But I should like to start as soon as possible."

"We shall go to-morrow morning," returned the Scarecrow. "So now let us all get ready, for it will be a long journey."

# Attacked by the Fighting Trees

THE next morning Dorothy kissed the pretty green girl good-bye, and they all shook hands with the soldier with the green whiskers, who had walked with them as far as the gate. When the Guardian of the Gates saw them again he wondered greatly that they could leave the beautiful City to get into new trouble. But he at once unlocked their spectacles, which he put back into the green box, and gave them many good wishes to carry with them.

"You are now our ruler," he said to the Scarecrow; "so you must come back to us as soon as possible."

"I certainly shall if I am able," the Scarecrow replied; "but I must help Dorothy to get home, first."

As Dorothy bade the good-natured Guardian a last farewell she said,

"I have been very kindly treated in your lovely City, and every-one has been good to me. I cannot tell you how grateful I am."

"Don't try, my dear," he answered. "We should like to keep you with us, but if it is your wish to return to Kansas I hope you will find a way." He then opened the gate of the outer wall and they walked forth and started upon their journey.

The sun shone brightly as our friends turned their faces toward the Land of the South. They were all in the best of spirits, and laughed and chatted together. Dorothy was once more filled with the hope of getting home, and the Scarecrow and the Tin Wood-man were glad to be of use to her. As for the Lion, he sniffed the fresh air with delight and whisked his tail from side to side in pure joy at being in the country again, while Toto ran around them and chased the moths and butterflies, barking merrily all the time.

"City life does not agree with me at all," remarked the Lion, as they walked along at a brisk pace. "I have lost much flesh since I lived there, and now I am anxious for a chance to show the other beasts how courageous I have grown."

They now turned and took a last look at the Emerald City. All they could see was a mass of towers and steeples behind the green walls, and high up above everything the spires and dome of the Palace of Oz.

"Oz was not such a bad Wizard, after all," said the Tin Woodman, as he felt his heart rattling around in his breast.

"He knew how to give me brains, and very good brains, too," said the Scarecrow.

"If Oz had taken a dose of the same courage he gave me," added the Lion, "he would have been a brave man."

Dorothy said nothing. Oz had not kept the promise he made her, but he had done his best, so she forgave him. As he said, he was a good man, even if he was a bad Wizard.

The first day's journey was through the green fields and bright flowers that stretched about the Emerald City on every side. They slept that night on the grass, with nothing but the stars over them; and they rested very well indeed.

In the morning they travelled on until they came to a thick wood. There was no way of going around it, for it seemed to extend to the right and left as far as they could see; and, besides, they did not dare change the direction of their journey for fear of getting lost. So they looked for the place where it would be easiest to get into the forest.

The Scarecrow, who was in the lead, finally discovered a big tree with such wide spreading branches that there was room for the party to pass underneath. So he walked forward to the tree, but just as he came under the first branches they bent down and twined around him, and the next minute he was raised from the ground and flung headlong among his fellow travellers.

This did not hurt the Scarecrow, but it surprised him, and he looked rather dizzy when Dorothy picked him up.

# Attacked by the Fighting Trees

"Here is another space between the trees," called the Lion.

"Let me try it first," said the Scarecrow, "for it doesn't hurt me to get thrown about." He walked up to another tree, as he spoke, but its branches immediately seized him and tossed him back again.

"This is strange," exclaimed Dorothy; "what shall we do?"

"The trees seem to have made up their minds to fight us, and stop our journey," remarked the Lion.

"I believe I will try it myself," said the Woodman, and shouldering his axe he marched up to the first tree that had handled the Scarecrow so roughly. When a big branch bent down to seize him the Woodman chopped at it so fiercely that he cut it in two. At once the tree began shaking all its branches as if in pain, and the Tin Woodman passed safely under it.

"Come on!" he shouted to the others; "be quick!"

They all ran forward and passed under the tree without injury, except Toto, who was caught by a small branch and shaken until he howled. But the Woodman promptly chopped off the branch and set the little dog free.

The other trees of the forest did nothing to keep them back, so they made up their minds that only the first row of trees could bend down their branches, and that probably these were the policemen of the forest, and given this wonderful power in order to keep strangers out of it.

The four travellers walked with ease through the trees until they came to the further edge of the wood. Then, to their surprise, they found before them a high wall, which seemed to be made of white china.[23] It was smooth, like the surface of a dish, and higher than their heads.

"What shall we do now?" asked Dorothy.

"I will make a ladder," said the Tin Woodman, "for we certainly must climb over the wall."

# The Dainty China Country

WHILE the Woodman was making a ladder from wood which he found in the forest Dorothy lay down and slept, for she was tired by the long walk. The Lion also curled himself up to sleep and Toto lay beside him.

The Scarecrow watched the Woodman while he worked, and said to him:

"I cannot think why this wall is here, nor what it is made of."

"Rest your brains and do not worry about the wall," replied the Woodman; "when we have climbed over it we shall know what is on the other side."

After a time the ladder was finished. It looked clumsy, but the Tin Woodman was sure it was strong and would answer their purpose. The Scarecrow waked Dorothy and the Lion and Toto, and told them that the ladder was ready. The Scarecrow climbed up the ladder first, but he was so awkward that Dorothy had to follow close behind and keep him from falling off.[24] When he got his head over the top of the wall the Scarecrow said,

"Oh, my!"

"Go on," exclaimed Dorothy.

So the Scarecrow climbed further up and sat down on the top of the wall, and Dorothy put her head over and cried,

"Oh, my!" just as the Scarecrow had done.

Then Toto came up, and immediately began to bark, but Dorothy made him be still.

The Lion climbed the ladder next, and the Tin Woodman came last; but both of them cried, "Oh, my!" as soon as they looked over the wall. When they were all sitting in a row on the top of the wall they looked down and saw a strange sight.

Before them was a great stretch of country having a floor as smooth and shining and white as the bottom of a big platter. Scattered around were many houses made entirely of china and painted in the brightest colors. These houses were quite small, the biggest of them reaching only as high as Dorothy's waist. There were also pretty little barns, with china fences around them, and many cows and sheep and horses and pigs and chickens, all made of china, were standing about in groups.

But the strangest of all were the people who lived in this queer country. There were milk-maids and shepherdesses, with bright-colored bodices and golden spots all over their gowns; and princesses with most gorgeous frocks of silver and gold and purple; and shepherds dressed in knee-breeches with pink and yellow and blue stripes down them, and golden buckles on their shoes; and princes with jewelled crowns upon their heads, wearing ermine robes and satin doublets; and funny clowns in ruffled gowns, with round red spots upon their cheeks and tall, pointed caps. And, strangest of all, these people were all made of china, even to their clothes, and were so small that the tallest of them was no higher than Dorothy's knee.

No one did so much as look at the travellers at first, except one little purple china dog with an extra-large head, which came to the wall and barked at them in a tiny voice, afterwards running away again.

"How shall we get down?" asked Dorothy.

They found the ladder so heavy they could not pull it up, so the Scarecrow fell off the wall and the others jumped down upon him so that the hard floor would not hurt their feet. Of course they took pains not to light on his head and get the pins in their feet. When all were safely down they picked up the Scarecrow, whose body was quite flattened out, and patted his straw into shape again.

"We must cross this strange place in order to get to the other side," said Dorothy; "for it would be unwise for us to go any other way except due South."

They began walking through the country of the china people, and the first thing they came to was a china milk-maid milking a china cow. As they drew near the cow suddenly gave a kick and kicked over the stool, the pail, and even the milk-maid herself, all falling on the china ground with a great clatter.

Dorothy was shocked to see that the cow had broken her leg short off, and that the pail was lying in several small pieces, while the poor milk-maid had a nick in her left elbow.

"There!" cried the milk-maid, angrily; "see what you have done! My cow has broken her leg, and I must take her to the mender's shop and have it glued on again. What do you mean by coming here and frightening my cow?"

"I'm very sorry," returned Dorothy; "please forgive us."

But the pretty milk-maid was much too vexed to make any answer. She picked up the leg sulkily and led her cow away, the poor animal limping on three legs. As she left them the milk-maid cast many reproachful glances over her shoulder at the clumsy strangers, holding her nicked elbow close to her side.

Dorothy was quite grieved at this mishap.

"We must be very careful here," said the kind-hearted Woodman, "or we may hurt these pretty little people so they will never get over it."

A little farther on Dorothy met a most beautiful dressed young princess, who stopped short as she saw the strangers and started to run away.

Dorothy wanted to see more of the princess, so she ran after her; but the china girl cried out,

"Don't chase me! don't chase me!"

She had such a frightened little voice that Dorothy stopped and said,

"Why not?"

"Because," answered the princess, also stopping, a safe distance away, "if I run I may fall down and break myself."

"But couldn't you be mended?" asked the girl.

"Oh, yes; but one is never so pretty after being mended, you know," replied the princess.

"I suppose not," said Dorothy.

"Now there is Mr. Joker, one of our clowns," continued the china lady, "who is always trying to stand upon his head. He has broken himself so often that he is mended in a hundred places, and doesn't look at all pretty. Here he comes now, so you can see for yourself."

Indeed, a jolly little Clown now came walking toward them, and Dorothy could see that in spite of his pretty clothes of red and yellow and green he was completely covered with cracks, running every which way and showing plainly that he had been mended in many places.

The Clown put his hands in his pockets, and after puffing out his cheeks and nodding his head at them saucily he said,

> "My lady fair,
> Why do you stare
> At poor old Mr. Joker?
> You're quite as stiff
> And prim as if
> You'd eaten up a poker!"

"Be quiet, sir!" said the princess; "can't you see these are strangers, and should be treated with respect?"

"Well, that's respect, I expect," declared the Clown, and immediately stood upon his head.

"Don't mind Mr. Joker," said the princess to Dorothy; "he is considerably cracked in his head, and that makes him foolish."

"Oh, I don't mind him a bit," said Dorothy. "But you are so beautiful," she continued, "that I am sure I could love you dearly. Won't you let me carry you back to Kansas and stand you on Aunt Em's mantle-shelf? I could carry you in my basket."

"That would make me very unhappy," answered the china princess. "You see, here in our own country we live contentedly, and can talk and move around as we please. But whenever any of us are taken away our joints at once stiffen, and we can only stand straight and look pretty. Of course that is all that is expected of us when we are on mantle-shelves and cabinets and drawing-room tables, but our lives are much pleasanter here in our own country."

"I would not make you unhappy for all the world!" exclaimed Dorothy; "so I'll just say good-bye."

"Good-bye," replied the princess.

They walked carefully through the china country. The little

animals and all the people scampered out of their way, fearing the strangers would break them, and after an hour or so the travellers reached the other side of the country and came to another china wall.

It was not as high as the first, however, and by standing upon the Lion's back they all managed to scramble to the top. Then the Lion gathered his legs under him and jumped on the wall; but just as he jumped he upset a china church with his tail and smashed it all to pieces.[25]

"That was too bad," said Dorothy, "but really I think we were lucky in not doing these little people more harm than breaking a cow's leg and a church. They are all so brittle!"

"They are, indeed," said the Scarecrow, "and I am thankful I am made of straw and cannot be easily damaged. There are worse things in the world than being a Scarecrow."

# The Lion Becomes
# the King of Beasts

AFTER climbing down from the china wall the travellers found themselves in a disagreeable country, full of bogs and marshes and covered with tall, rank grass. It was difficult to walk far without falling into muddy holes, for the grass was so thick that it hid them from sight. However, by carefully picking their way, they got safely along until they reached solid ground. But here the country seemed wilder than ever, and after a long and tiresome walk through the underbrush they entered another forest, where the trees were bigger and older than any they had ever seen.

"This forest is perfectly delightful," declared the Lion, looking around him with joy; "never have I seen a more beautiful place."

"It seems gloomy," said the Scarecrow.

"Not a bit of it," answered the Lion; "I should like to live here all my life. See how soft the dried leaves are under your feet and how rich and green the moss is that clings to these old trees. Surely no wild beast could wish a pleasanter home."

"Perhaps there are wild beasts in the forest now," said Dorothy.

"I suppose there are," returned the Lion; "but I do not see any of them about."

They walked through the forest until it became too dark to go any farther. Dorothy and Toto and the Lion lay down to sleep, while the Woodman and the Scarecrow kept watch over them as usual.

When morning came they started again. Before they had gone far they heard a low rumble, as of the growling of many wild animals. Toto whimpered a little but none of the others was frightened and they kept along the well-trodden path until they came to an opening in the wood, in which were gathered hundreds of beasts of every variety. There were tigers and elephants and bears and wolves and foxes and all the others in the natural history, and for a moment Dorothy was afraid. But the Lion explained that the animals were holding a meeting, and he judged by their snarling and growling that they were in great trouble.

As he spoke several of the beasts caught sight of him, and at once the great assemblage hushed as if by magic. The biggest of the tigers came up to the Lion and bowed, saying,

"Welcome, O King of Beasts! You have come in good time to fight our enemy and bring peace to all the animals of the forest once more."

"What is your trouble?" asked the Lion, quietly.

"We are all threatened," answered the tiger, "by a fierce enemy which has lately come into this forest. It is a most tremendous monster, like a great spider, with a body as big as an elephant and legs as long as a tree trunk. It has eight of these long legs, and as the monster crawls through the forest he seizes an animal with a leg and drags it to his mouth, where he eats it as a spider does a fly. Not one of us is safe while this fierce creature is alive, and we had called a meeting to decide how to take care of ourselves when you came among us."

The Lion thought for a moment.

"Are there any other lions in this forest?" he asked.

"No; there were some, but the monster has eaten them all. And, besides, they were none of them nearly so large and brave as you."

"If I put an end to your enemy will you bow down to me and obey me as King of the Forest?" enquired the Lion.

"We will do that gladly," returned the tiger; and all the other beasts roared with a mighty roar: "We will!"

"Where is this great spider of yours now?" asked the Lion.

"Yonder, among the oak trees," said the tiger, pointing with his fore-foot.

"Take good care of these friends of mine," said the Lion, "and I will go at once to fight the monster."

# The Lion Becomes the King of Beasts

He bade his comrades good-bye and marched proudly away to do battle with the enemy.

The great spider was lying asleep when the Lion found him, and it looked so ugly that its foe turned up his nose in disgust. Its legs were quite as long as the tiger had said and its body covered with coarse black hair. It had a great mouth, with a row of sharp teeth a foot long; but its head was joined to the pudgy body by a neck as slender as a wasp's waist. This gave the Lion a hint of the best way to attack the creature, and as he knew it was easier to fight it asleep than awake, he gave a great spring and landed directly upon the monster's back. Then, with one blow of his heavy paw, all armed with sharp claws, he knocked the spider's head from its body. Jumping down, he watched it until the long legs stopped wiggling, when he knew it was quite dead.

The Lion went back to the opening where the beasts of the forest were waiting for him and said, proudly,

"You need fear your enemy no longer."

Then the beasts bowed down to the Lion as their King, and he promised to come back and rule over them as soon as Dorothy was safely on her way to Kansas.

# The Country of the Quadlings

THE four travellers passed through the rest of the forest in safety, and when they came out from its gloom saw before them a steep hill, covered from top to bottom with great pieces of rock.

"That will be a hard climb," said the Scarecrow, "but we must get over the hill, nevertheless."

So he led the way and the others followed. They had nearly reached the first rock when they heard a rough voice cry out,

"Keep back!"

"Who are you?" asked the Scarecrow. Then a head showed itself over the rock and the same voice said,

"This hill belongs to us, and we don't allow anyone to cross it."

"But we must cross it," said the Scarecrow. "We're going to the country of the Quadlings."

"But you shall not!" replied the voice, and there stepped from behind the rock the strangest man the travellers had ever seen.

He was quite short and stout and had a big head, which was flat at the top and supported by a thick neck full of wrinkles. But he had no arms at all, and, seeing this, the Scarecrow did not fear that so helpless a creature could prevent them from climbing the hill. So he said,

"I'm sorry not to do as you wish, but we must pass over your hill whether you like it or not," and he walked boldly forward.

As quick as lightning the man's head shot forward and his neck stretched out until the top of the head, where it was flat, struck the Scarecrow in the middle and sent him tumbling, over and over, down the hill. Almost as quickly as it came the head went back to the body, and the man laughed harshly as he said,

"It isn't as easy as you think!"

A chorus of boisterous laughter came from the other rocks, and Dorothy saw hundreds of the armless Hammer-Heads upon the hillside, one behind every rock.

The Lion became quite angry at the laughter caused by the Scarecrow's mishap, and giving a loud roar that echoed like thunder he dashed up the hill.

Again a head shot swiftly out, and the great Lion went rolling down the hill as if he had been struck by a cannon ball.

Dorothy ran down and helped the Scarecrow to his feet, and the Lion came up to her, feeling rather bruised and sore, and said,

"It is useless to fight people with shooting heads; no one can withstand them."

"What can we do, then?" she asked.

"Call the Winged Monkeys," suggested the Tin Woodman; "you have still the right to command them once more."

"Very well," she answered, and putting on the Golden Cap she uttered the magic words. The Monkeys were as prompt as ever, and in a few moments the entire band stood before her.

"What are your commands?" enquired the King of the Monkeys, bowing low.

"Carry us over the hill to the country of the Quadlings," answered the girl.

"It shall be done," said the King, and at once the Winged Monkeys caught the four travellers and Toto up in their arms and flew away with them. As they passed over the hill the Hammer-Heads yelled with vexation, and shot their heads high in the air; but they could not reach the Winged Monkeys, which carried Dorothy and her comrades safely over the hill and set them down in the beautiful country of the Quadlings.[26]

"This is the last time you can summon us," said the leader to Dorothy; "so good-bye and good luck to you."

"Good-bye, and thank you very much," returned the girl; and the Monkeys rose into the air and were out of sight in a twinkling.

The country of the Quadlings seemed rich and happy. There was field upon field of ripening grain, with well-paved roads running between, and pretty rippling brooks with strong bridges across them. The fences and houses and bridges were all painted

# The Country of the Quadlings

bright red, just as they had been painted yellow in the country of the Winkies and blue in the country of the Munchkins. The Quadlings themselves, who were short and fat and looked chubby and good natured, were dressed all in red, which showed bright against the green grass and the yellowing grain.

The Monkeys had set them down near a farm house, and the four travellers walked up to it and knocked at the door. It was opened by the farmer's wife, and when Dorothy asked for something to eat the woman gave them all a good dinner, with three kinds of cake and four kinds of cookies, and a bowl of milk for Toto.

"How far is it to the Castle of Glinda?" asked the child.

"It is not a great way," answered the farmer's wife. "Take the road to the South and you will soon reach it."

Thanking the good woman, they started afresh and walked by the fields and across the pretty bridges until they saw before them a very beautiful Castle. Before the gates were three young girls, dressed in handsome red uniforms trimmed with gold braid; and as Dorothy approached one of them said to her,

"Why have you come to the South Country?"

"To see the Good Witch who rules here," she answered. "Will you take me to her?"

"Let me have your name and I will ask Glinda if she will receive you." They told who they were, and the girl soldier went into the Castle. After a few moments she came back to say that Dorothy and the others were to be admitted at once.

*"You must give me the Golden Cap."*

# The Good Witch Grants Dorothy's Wish

BEFORE they went to see Glinda, however, they were taken to a room of the Castle, where Dorothy washed her face and combed her hair, and the Lion shook the dust out of his mane, and the Scarecrow patted himself into his best shape, and the Woodman polished his tin and oiled his joints.

When they were all quite presentable they followed the soldier girl into a big room where the Witch Glinda sat upon a throne of rubies.

She was both beautiful and young to their eyes. Her hair was a rich red in color and fell in flowing ringlets over her shoulders. Her dress was pure white; but her eyes were blue, and they looked kindly upon the little girl.

"What can I do for you, my child?" she asked.

Dorothy told the Witch all her story; how the cyclone had brought her to the Land of Oz, how she had found her companions, and of the wonderful adventures they had met with.

"My greatest wish now," she added, "is to get back to Kansas, for Aunt Em will surely think something dreadful has happened to me, and that will make her put on mourning; and unless the crops are better this year than they were last I am sure Uncle Henry cannot afford it."

Glinda leaned foward and kissed the sweet, upturned face of the loving little girl.

"Bless your dear heart," she said, "I am sure I can tell you of a way to get back to Kansas." Then she added:

"But, if I do, you must give me the Golden Cap."

"Willingly!" exclaimed Dorothy; "indeed, it is of no use to me now, and when you have it you can command the Winged Monkeys three times."

"And I think I shall need their service just those three times," answered Glinda, smiling.

Dorothy then gave her the Golden Cap, and the Witch said to the Scarecrow,

"What will you do when Dorothy has left us?"

"I will return to the Emerald City," he replied, "for Oz has made me its ruler and the people like me. The only thing that worries me is how to cross the hill of the Hammer-Heads."

"By means of the Golden Cap I shall command the Winged Monkeys to carry you to the gates of the Emerald City," said Glinda, "for it would be a shame to deprive the people of so wonderful a ruler."

"Am I really wonderful?" asked the Scarecrow.

"You are unusual," replied Glinda.

Turning to the Tin Woodman, she asked:

"What will become of you when Dorothy leaves this country?"

He leaned on his axe and thought a moment. Then he said, "The Winkies were very kind to me, and wanted me to rule over them after the Wicked Witch died. I am fond of the Winkies, and if I could get back again to the country of the West I should like nothing better than to rule over them forever."

"My second command to the Winged Monkeys," said Glinda, "will be that they carry you safely to the land of the Winkies. Your brains may not be so large to look at as those of the Scarecrow, but you are really brighter than he is—when you are well polished—and I am sure you will rule the Winkies wisely and well."

Then the Witch looked at the big, shaggy Lion and asked, "When Dorothy has returned to her own home, what will become of you?"

"Over the hill of the Hammer-Heads," he answered, "lies a grand old forest, and all the beasts that live there have made me their King. If I could only get back to this forest I would pass my life very happily there."

# The Good Witch Grants Dorothy's Wish

"My third command to the Winged Monkeys," said Glinda, "shall be to carry you to your forest. Then, having used up the powers of the Golden Cap, I shall give it the King of the Monkeys, that he and his band may thereafter be free for evermore."

The Scarecrow and the Tin Woodman and the Lion now thanked the Good Witch earnestly for her kindness, and Dorothy exclaimed,

"You are certainly as good as you are beautiful! But you have not yet told me how to get back to Kansas."

"Your silver shoes will carry you over the desert," replied Glinda. "If you had known their power you could have gone back to your Aunt Em the very first day you came to this country."

"But then I should not have had my wonderful brains!" cried the Scarecrow. "I might have passed my whole life in the farmer's cornfield."

"And I should not have had my lovely heart," said the Tin Woodman. "I might have stood and rusted in the forest till the end of the world."

"And I should have lived a coward forever," declared the Lion, "and no beast in all the forest would have had a good word to say to me."

"This is all true," said Dorothy, "and I am glad I was of use to these good friends. But now that each of them has had what he most desired, and each is happy in having a kingdom to rule beside, I think I should like to go back to Kansas."

"The silver shoes," said the Good Witch, "have wonderful powers. And one of the most curious things about them is that they can carry you to any place in the world in three steps, and each step will be made in the wink of an eye. All you have to do is to knock the heels together three times and command the shoes to carry you wherever you wish to go."

"If that is so," said the child, joyfully, "I will ask them to carry me back to Kansas at once."

She threw her arms around the Lion's neck and kissed him, patting his big head tenderly. Then she kissed the Tin Woodman, who was weeping in a way most dangerous to his joints. But she hugged the soft, stuffed body of the Scarecrow in her arms instead of kissing his painted face, and found she was crying herself at this sorrowful parting from her loving comrades.

Glinda the Good stepped down from her ruby throne to give the little girl a good-bye kiss, and Dorothy thanked her for all the kindness she had shown to her friends and herself.

Dorothy now took Toto up solemnly in her arms, and having said one last good-bye she clapped the heels of her shoes together three times, saying,

"Take me home to Aunt Em!"

\* \* \* \* \*

Instantly she was whirling through the air, so swiftly that all she could see or feel was the wind whistling past her ear.

The silver shoes took but three steps, and then she stopped so suddenly that she rolled over upon the grass several times before she knew where she was.

At length, however, she sat up and looked about her.

"Good gracious!" she cried.

For she was sitting on the broad Kansas prairie, and just before her was the new farm-house Uncle Henry built after the cyclone had carried away the old one. Uncle Henry was milking the cows in the barnyard, and Toto had jumped out of her arms and was running toward the barn, barking joyously.

Dorothy stood up and found she was in her stocking-feet. For the silver shoes had fallen off in her flight through the air, and were lost forever in the desert.

# Home Again

AUNT Em had just come out of the house to water the cabbages when she looked up and saw Dorothy running toward her.

"My darling child!" she cried, folding the little girl in her arms and covering her face with kisses; "where in the world did you come from?"

"From the Land of Oz," said Dorothy, gravely. "And here is Toto, too. And oh, Aunt Em! I'm so glad to be at home again!"

*Notes and Bibliography*

# Notes

1. The word "gray" appears nine times in the space of four paragraphs. Baum is clearly contrasting the grayness of life on the Kansas farm, and the solemnity of Uncle Henry and Aunt Em, with the color and gaiety of Oz.

2. One of Professor Woggle-Bug's most inexcusable errors was to place the Munchkin region on the west and the Winkie country on the east of his map of Oz.

3. It was not until the Royal Historian wrote his second Oz book that he learned the name and color of the northern area—the purple country of the Gillikins.

4. In *The Patchwork Girl of Oz* (p. 163) we learn of the second road of yellow brick. Both roads are in Munchkin country, but quite distinct from each other.

5. Dorothy may still have this key. It would be interesting to know if the old farm house is still standing at the spot where the cyclone left it.

6. Both Denslow and Neill always drew the Scarecrow with a larger left eye, showing a respect for the text of the Royal History that has not been shared by other Oz illustrators.

7. The many references in this story to the deaths of men and beasts are hard to reconcile with our later knowledge concerning the extreme difficulty of "destroying" living beings in Oz.

8. Not until the twelfth book of the series, *The Tin Woodman of Oz,* does the tin man attempt to fulfil his obligation to return to his former sweetheart (her name is Nimmie Amee)

and offer marriage. He finds her happily wedded to Chopfyte, a composite man assembled by the tinsmith (Ku-Klip) from the former bodies of the Tin Woodman (whose name had been Nick Chopper), and the Tin Soldier (formerly Captain Fyter). Captain Fyter had also wooed the Munchkin maiden, only to meet with the same unfortunate fate as her former suitor. The histories of these two remarkable personages raise profound metaphysical questions concerning personal identity.

9. The Kalidahs are encountered on one other occasion in the Royal History, by Trot, Cap'n Bill, and the Glass Cat in *The Magic of Oz,* p. 104f.

10. This and other passages in the book reveal that the Royal Historian was not yet aware of the extent to which fauna and flora in Oz bear the same color as the region in which they flourish.

11. In *Tik-Tok of Oz* (p. 268) we discover that Toto was capable of speaking the moment he entered Oz. He just didn't feel like it.

12. Money in Oz? Perhaps under the Wizard's rule children in the Emerald City were permitted to carry token pennies.

13. Her name is given in the second Oz book—Jellia Jamb.

14. The Wizard failed to keep this promise. We learn in *The Tin Woodman of Oz* (p. 31) that it was a "kind" but not a "loving" heart.

15. My wife has called my attention to the close similarity of this incantation to "ipecac," the name of a once popular household emetic still sold in drugstores.

16. This little queen and twelve of her subjects play an important role in the second Oz book in helping the Scarecrow regain his throne.

17. Nothing is known of Gayelette's subsequent history.

18. We learn more about the Wizard's former life in *Dorothy and the Wizard in Oz* (p. 192f). His real name was Oscar Zoroaster Phadrig Isaac Norman Henkle Emmannuel Ambroise Diggs. Because his initials spelled "pinhead," he dropped all the names except the first two. When he first

arrived in Oz the natives, seeing "O. Z." on his balloon, naturally supposed him to be their rightful ruler.

19. The Wizard is being over-modest and slightly untruthful.
When he built the Emerald City he used more emeralds than
any other precious stone. The practice of wearing green spectacles was never really necessary, and was discontinued soon
after the Wizard left the throne.

20. Either the Wizard imagined he had aged or he was already
elderly when he left the United States, for no one ages in Oz.

21. Silk velvet, as we learn in *The Tin Woodman of Oz* (p. 230).

22. "So far as they knew." The Royal Historian obviously implies
that there may be a good many rulers outside of Oz who are
stuffed figures.

23. *Cf.* the Great Wall of China.

24. The Scarecrow's tumble down the rungs of a ladder was one
of the comic highlights of Fred Stone's performance in the
stage version of this book.

25. The only reference in the Royal History to a church in Oz.

26. At this time, apparently, the borders of the Quadling country did not extend northward as far as the green marble wall
surrounding the Emerald City (*Cf. The Patchwork Girl of
Oz*, p. 184).

# Bibliography

## L. FRANK BAUM

1886 *The Book of the Hamburgs; a Brief Treatise Upon the Mating, Rearing and Management of the Different Varieties of Hamburgs.* Hartford, Conn.: H. H. Stoddard. Baum's first published book, paper covers, 71 pages. A "chicken fancier" all his life, Baum won many prizes for chickens that he bred and entered in competitions.

1897 *Mother Goose in Prose.* Chicago: Way and Williams. Illustrated by Maxfield Parrish. Twenty-two stories, each based on a Mother Goose rhyme. Dorothy, a little farm girl, appears in the last story, but when the story was later reprinted (in *The Snuggle Tales* series, 1916) Baum changed her name to Doris.

1898 *By the Candelabra's Glare.* Chicago: Privately Printed by L. Frank Baum in an edition of 99 copies. Forty-one poems illustrated by W. W. Denslow and others.

1899 *Father Goose, His Book.* Chicago: George M. Hill. Nonsense verse illustrated by Denslow.

1900 *The Songs of Father Goose.* Chicago: George M. Hill. Illustrated by Denslow. Verses from Father Goose set to music by Alberta N. Burton.
*The Art of Decorating Dry Goods Windows and Interiors.* Chicago: The Show Window Publishing Co.
*The Army Alphabet.* Chicago: George M. Hill. Illustrated by Harry Kennedy.
*The Navy Alphabet.* Chicago: George M. Hill. Illustrated by Kennedy.

*A New Wonderland.* New York: R. H. Russell. Illustrated by Frank Verbeck. Fourteen amusing tales about the Beautiful Valley of Phunnyland. Reissued by Bobbs-Merrill in 1903 as *The Surprising Adventures of the Magical Monarch of Mo* with "Mo" substituted for "Phunnyland" throughout the text and a rewritten first chapter. Letters of Baum leave no doubt that this book was conceived and written before he wrote *The Wizard.*

*The Wonderful Wizard of Oz.* Chicago: George M. Hill. Illustrated by Denslow.

1901 *Dot and Tot of Merryland.* Chicago: George M. Hill. Illustrated by Denslow.

*American Fairy Tales.* Chicago: George M. Hill. Illustrated by Ike Morgan and others.

*The Master Key.* Indianapolis: Bowen-Merrill. Illustrated by Fanny Cory. A science fiction novel about the future wonders of electricity.

1902 *The Life and Adventures of Santa Claus.* Indianapolis: Bowen-Merrill. Illustrated by Mary Cowles Clark.

1903 *The Enchanted Island of Yew.* Indianapolis: Bobbs-Merrill. Illustrated by Fanny Y. Cory.

1904 *The Marvelous Land of Oz.* Chicago: Reilly and Britton. This and all subsequent Oz books are illustrated by John R. Neill.

1905 *Queen Zixi of Ix.* New York: Century. Illustrated by Frederick Richardson. A magic cloak provides fulfilment of one wish for each wearer. The story was first serialized in *St. Nicholas* in 1904 and 1905.

*The Woggle-Bug Book.* Chicago: Reilly and Britton. Illustrated by Ike Morgan. A large paper-backed book about the Woggle-Bug's misfortunes in an American City.

1906 *John Dough and the Cherub.* Chicago: Reilly and Britton. Illustrated by Neill. The Adventures of John Dough, a huge gingerbread man, and his companion, Chick the Cherub. Chick is the world's first incubator baby. His (or her) sex is never revealed. A Chicago newspaper offered a prize for the best reason for thinking Chick a boy or girl, and contest blanks were inserted in the first issue of the book.

1907    *Ozma of Oz.* Chicago: Reilly and Britton.
*Father Goose's Year Book: Quaint Quacks and Feathered Shafts for Mature Children.* Chicago: Reilly and Britton. Illustrated by Walter J. Enright. A collection of poems and epigrams by Baum.

1908    *Baum's American Fairy Tales.* Indianapolis: Bobbs-Merrill. Illustrated by George Kerr. A reissue of *American Fairy Tales,* containing three additional stories and a new preface.
*Dorothy and the Wizard in Oz.* Chicago: Reilly and Britton.

1909    *The Road to Oz.* Chicago: Reilly and Britton.

1910    *The Emerald City of Oz.* Chicago: Reilly and Britton.
*L. Frank Baum's Juvenile Speaker.* Chicago: Reilly and Britton. Verse and prose selections from Baum's works, and a previously unpublished playlet. Introduction by Baum.

1911    *The Sea Fairies.* Chicago: Reilly and Britton. Illustrated by Neill. The undersea adventures of Trot, a California girl, and her companion Cap'n Bill.
*The Daring Twins.* Chicago: Reilly and Britton.

1912    *Sky Island.* Chicago: Reilly and Britton. Illustrated by Neill. A magic umbrella carries Trot, Cap'n Bill, and Button-Bright to an island in the sky.
*Baum's Own Book for Children.* Chicago: Reilly and Britton. Reissue of *L. Frank Baum's Juvenile Speaker,* save for the introduction, which is omitted.
*Phoebe Daring.* Chicago: Reilly and Britton.

1913    *The Patchwork Girl of Oz.* Chicago: Reilly and Britton.
*Jack Pumpkinhead and the Sawhorse, Little Dorothy and Toto, Ozma and the Little Wizard, The Cowardly Lion and the Hungry Tiger, The Scarecrow and the Tin Woodman, and Tiktok and the Nome King.* Chicago: Reilly and Britton. Illustrated by Neill. Six separate booklets, each a complete story. These are Baum's only short stories about Oz, introducing some characters not to be found in any Oz book. Reissued in 1914 as a single volume.

1914 *Tik-Tok of Oz.* Chicago: Reilly and Britton.
*Little Wizard Stories of Oz.* Chicago: Reilly and Britton. Reissue as a single volume of the short stories published the previous year.

1915 *The Scarecrow of Oz.* Chicago: Reilly and Britton.

1916 *Rinkitink in Oz.* Chicago: Reilly and Britton.
*The Snuggle Tales.* Chicago: Reilly and Britton. Six small books containing excerpts from the Oz books and some verse from *Father Goose.* Reissued in 1920 under the general title of *Oz-Man Tales.*

1917 *The Lost Princess of Oz.* Chicago: Reilly and Britton.

1918 *The Tin Woodman of Oz.* Chicago: Reilly and Britton.

1919 *The Magic of Oz.* Chicago: Reilly and Lee.

1920 *Glinda of Oz.* Chicago: Reilly and Lee.

1941 *Our Landlady.* Mitchell, South Dakota: South Dakota Federal Writers' Project. A selection of Baum's columns from the *Aberdeen Saturday Pioneer,* a newspaper he edited in Aberdeen, South Dakota.

1953 *Jaglon and the Tiger Fairies.* Chicago: Reilly and Lee. Illustrated by Dale Ulrey, text expanded by Jack Snow. First in a projected series of book editions of nine "animal fairy tales" (as Baum called them) that first appeared in *The Delineator* in 1905.

## ANONYMOUS AND PSEUDONYMOUS WORKS

### ANONYMOUS

1908 *The Last Egyptian.* Philadelphia: Edward Stern. A romantic adult novel about modern Egypt.

### FLOYD AKERS

1908 *The Boy Fortune Hunters in Alaska.* Chicago: Reilly and Britton. Reissue of *Sam Steele's Adventures on Land and Sea,* by Capt. Hugh Fitzgerald.
*The Boy Fortune Hunters in Panama.* Chicago: Reilly and Britton. Reissue of *Sam Steele's Adventures in Panama,* by Capt. Hugh Fitzgerald.

# Bibliography

*The Boy Fortune Hunters in Egypt.* Chicago: Reilly and Britton.

1909 *The Boy Fortune Hunters in China.* Chicago: Reilly and Britton.

1910 *The Boy Fortune Hunters in Yucatan.* Chicago: Reilly and Britton.

1911 *The Boy Fortune Hunters in the South Seas.* Chicago: Reilly and Britton.

## LAURA BANCROFT

1906 *Bandit Jim Crow, Mr. Woodchuck, Prairie-Dog Town, Prince Mud-Turtle, Sugar-Loaf Mountain,* and *Twinkle's Enchantment.* Chicago: Reilly and Britton. Illustrated by Maginel Wright Enright. Six fantasy tales issued as six small books. Reissued as a single volume in 1911.
*Policeman Bluejay.* Chicago: Reilly and Britton. Illustrated by Enright. Two children acquire the bodies of birds and enter a nature fairyland. Reissued in 1911 as *Babes in Birdland.* Again reissued in 1917 as *Babes in Birdland* with Baum's name on the title page, and with an introduction by him, here first printed.

1911 *Twinkle and Chubbins.* Chicago: Reilly and Britton. Reissue in one volume of the six fantasy tales.

## JOHN ESTES COOKE

1907 *Tamawaca Folks.* Tamawaca Press. A privately issued novel of 99 copies, about Baum's friends in the Macatawa resort area.

## CAPT. HUGH FITZGERALD

1906 *Sam Steele's Adventures on Land and Sea.* Chicago: Reilly and Britton. (Cover title: *Sam Steele's Adventures.*)

1907 *Sam Steele's Adventures in Panama.* Chicago: Reilly and Britton.

## SUZANNE METCALF

1906 *Annabel.* Chicago: Reilly and Britton.

## SCHUYLER STAUNTON

1905 *The Fate of a Crown.* Chicago: Reilly and Britton. Romantic adult novel set in Brazil.

1906 *Daughters of Destiny.* Chicago: Reilly and Britton. Romantic adult novel set in Baluchistan.

## EDITH VAN DYNE

1906 *Aunt Jane's Nieces.* Chicago: Reilly and Britton
*Aunt Jane's Nieces Abroad.* Chicago: Reilly and Britton.

1908 *Aunt Jane's Nieces at Millville.* Chicago: Reilly and Britton.

1909 *Aunt Jane's Nieces at Work.* Chicago: Reilly and Britton.

1910 *Aunt Jane's Nieces in Society.* Chicago: Reilly and Britton.

1911 *Aunt Jane's Nieces and Uncle John.* Chicago: Reilly and Britton.
*The Flying Girl.* Chicago: Reilly and Britton.

1912 *Aunt Jane's Nieces on Vacation.* Chicago: Reilly and Britton.
*The Flying Girl and Her Chum.* Chicago: Reilly and Britton.

1913 *Aunt Jane's Nieces on the Ranch.* Chicago: Reilly and Britton.

1914 *Aunt Jane's Nieces Out West.* Chicago: Reilly and Britton.

1915 *Aunt Jane's Nieces in the Red Cross.* Chicago: Reilly and Britton.

1916 *Mary Louise.* Chicago: Reilly and Britton.
*Mary Louise in the Country.* Chicago: Reilly and Britton.

1917 *Mary Louise Solves a Mystery.* Chicago: Reilly and Britton.

1918 *Mary Louise and the Liberty Girls.* Chicago: Reilly and Britton.

1919 *Mary Louise Adopts a Soldier.* Chicago: Reilly and Lee.

### INTRODUCTIONS

1905 *Christmas Stocking Series.* Chicago: Reilly and Britton. Six booklets of well known stories and poems, all containing the same preface by Baum. The preface was reprinted in

*Land of Play,* edited by Sara T. Lefferts, 1911, New York: Cupples and Leon.

1907 *In Other Lands than Ours.* Chicago: Privately Printed. A collection of letters written by Mrs. L. Frank Baum while she and her husband were abroad. Frontispiece photograph of Mrs. Baum and sixteen photographs taken on the trip.

### CONTRIBUTIONS TO ANTHOLOGIES

1907 *Sweethearts Always,* edited by Janet Madison. Chicago: Reilly and Britton. Contains Baum's poem, "Her Answer."

1909 *The Loving Cup,* edited by Wilbur D. Nesbit. Chicago: P. F. Volland. Contains a poem by Baum titled "Smile," not published elsewhere.

### MAGAZINE STORIES NEVER REPRINTED IN BOOK FORM

1897 "The Suicide of Kiaros," *The White Elephant,* Sept. A locked-room murder mystery. Reprinted in *Ellery Queen's Mystery Magazine,* Nov., 1954, with a delightful introduction by Fred Dannay praising the "irresistible vistas" of Oz.

1898 "The Mating Day," *Short Stories,* Sept.

1900 "The Loveridge Burglary," *Short Stories.* Jan.

1904 "A Kidnapped Santa Claus," *Delineator,* Dec.

1905 "Animal Fairy Tales," a series of nine stories, illustrated by Charles Livingston Bull. *Delineator,* Jan. through Sept. "Jack Burgitt's Honor," *Novelettes,* No. 68, Aug.

1910 "Juggerjook," *St. Nicholas,* Dec.

1912 "Aunt Phroney's Boy," *St. Nicholas,* Dec.

### REFERENCES ABOUT BAUM

"L. Frank Baum and His New Plays," by D. E. Kessler, *The Theatre,* Aug., 1909. Baum is reported working on three new musicals: *The Pipes O' Pan, Ozma of Oz,* and *Peter and Paul.* Only the first was completed, though never produced. The original manuscript is owned by Frank J. Baum who also possesses the manuscript of *The Girl from Oz,* another unproduced Baum musical.

*Early Days in Dakota,* by Edwin C. Torrey, 1925. Minneapolis: Parnham Printing and Stationery Co. A brief chapter is devoted to Baum.

*Utopia Americana,* by Edward Wagenknecht, 1929. Seattle: University of Washington Bookstore. This booklet was the first critical study of Baum's work.

"The Wizard of Chittenango," by James Thurber, *The New Republic,* Dec. 12, 1934.

*The World at My Shoulder,* By Eunice Tietjens, 1938, p. 14f. New York: Macmillan.

"The Man Who Invented Oz," by Jeanne O. Potter, *Los Angeles Times Sunday Magazine,* August 13, 1939.

"Why the Wizard of Oz Keeps on Selling," by Frank Baum (son of L. Frank Baum), *Writer's Digest,* Dec., 1952.

*Who's Who in Oz,* by Jack Snow, 1954. Chicago: Reilly and Lee.

"The Wizard of Oz," by Vincent Starrett, in *Best Loved Books of the Twentieth Century,* 1955. New York: Bantam.

"L. Frank Baum and the 'Oz Books,'" by Roland Baughman, *Columbia Library Columns,* May, 1955. A perceptive appreciation by the head of the special collections department of Columbia University Libraries.

*L. Frank Baum. The Wonderful Wizard of Oz,* 1956. New York: Columbia University Libraries. A 50-page record of an exhibit at Columbia University of Baum's published writings. Introduction by Roland Baughman and descriptive notes by Baughman and Joan Baum, his assistant.

"The Oz Film Co.," by Frank Baum, *Films in Review,* Aug.-Sept., 1956.

*Cyclopedia of American Biography,* New Edition, Vol. 10, p. 168.

*National Cyclopedia of American Biography,* Vol. 18, p.331.

*Dictionary of American Biography,* Vol. 2, p. 59.

*Encyclopedia of American Biography,* New Series, Vol. 6, p. 378.